*Every Day I Bless You*

# Every Day I Bless You

## Reflections on the Healing Power of Shiva

NORMAN J. FRIED, PhD

URIM PUBLICATIONS
Jerusalem • New York

Every Day I Bless You: Reflections on the Healing Power of Shiva
*by* Norman J. Fried

Copyright © 2012 by Norman J. Fried

Book design by Ariel Walden

*Printed in Israel*
First Edition

ISBN 978-965-524-077-1

Urim Publications
P.O.Box 52287
Jerusalem 91521 Israel

Lambda Publishers, Inc.
527 Empire Blvd.
Brooklyn, NY 11225 U.S.A.
Tel: 718-972-5449, fax: 718-972-6307

www.UrimPublications.com

# Contents

*For my mother, Selma M. Fried,*

*And for Beth, my beloved*

# Acknowledgements

THE THEORIES I offer in this book reflect the integration of study and practice inspired by many great thinkers in the disciplines of religion, philosophy and psychology. In particular, interested readers are referred to the religious and existential writings of Rabbi Joseph Soloveitchik (1903–1993). Rabbi Soloveitchik, or *The Rav* as he was commonly known, was one of the leading Talmudic scholars of the twentieth century. His lectures and writings provided a strong foundation upon which many of my essays were built. In addition, my exegesis on Jacob wrestling with the angel in Chapter 3 (Ire) was inspired by my friend and teacher, Rabbi Alan B. Lucas of Temple Beth Sholom in New York.

I wish to acknowledge Jeni Friedman, a dear friend and colleague, and doctoral student at NYU Steinhardt Education & Jewish Studies. Jeni read and edited the many versions of *Every Day I Bless You* as they were being written, and guided me with her expansive knowledge of Jewish law and Scripture.

Thank you to Siegfried Schaffer, who listened and supported me in my beginning hours of sorrow. Scott Fried, Stephanie Mark, Dr. Barbara Hirsch, Deborah Levinson, Randi Marcus and Susan Jacobson also deserve recognition. Their personal experiences with *shiva* served as my guide as I studied the varying forms that this traditional mourning process can take.

A special thank you goes to Kristen Saberito Carter whose expertise in graphic design enhanced Kristina Swarner's beautiful cover illustration.

My Three sons, Joshua, Jacob and David are my deepest inspiration and my best friends. I honor them here as I do every day.

Finally, I wish to thank Tzvi Mauer at Urim Publications who believed in *Every Day I Bless You* enough to publish it.

— N. J. F., Manhasset, New York, USA
9 Elul 5771

# Introduction

For centuries, man has struggled with the concept of death and with the rituals that follow in its aftermath. And as our generations pass, we struggle still. In words apocryphal or mundane, spiritual or skeptical, we reason with ourselves or we wrestle with our God. We conjoin intellect with faith, psychology with spirituality, science with religion, only to remain uncertain or unwilling to accept the inevitable. Our beliefs about death vary across culture and religion, and they change sometimes throughout the course of a life. Many of us consider death to be a "termination" or cessation of all life energy: an absolute without memorial. Others think of death as a "doorway" to another way of being, an existential or spiritual portal to a timeless "other world."

The Jewish Bible does not explore the subject of death in depth, except to record it as an inevitable part of the life cycle of our matriarchs and patriarchs, the prophets, their disciples, and the generations that followed. Jewish tradition, however, has indeed developed rituals to which a mourner must adhere. These rituals, and mourning rites, occur in five graduated periods of time, or "phases," during which we, the bereaved, can express our sorrow in a controlled and structured manner.

Perhaps the most well-known of these phases is the period of *shiva* (from the Hebrew word for "seven"). This stage, or phase, lasts for the first seven days that follow the burial of a loved one. The observance of *shiva* is traced back to biblical times, when Abraham "rose up" after his wife, Sarah's, death (Genesis 23:3). The first account of the length of the traditional mourning period appears later in Genesis, when Joseph mourned seven days after his father's death (50:10). During these days, acquaintances, friends and relatives visit with the bereaved. They offer us comfort and compassion as we talk about our loss. The world remains smaller to us during these days. In our isolation from the ordinary duties of the week, we retreat inward, expressing our grief through observances of prayer, sitting on the floor or upon a low stool, and wearing a rent garment, or ribbon, as a symbol of our torn heart.

Though the days of *shiva* are seven, containing a distinct beginning and a certain end, the days of our mourning continue indefinitely, always searching for resolution. How we manage through our days, and the lessons we learn along the way, are our perpetual bounty to work with toward growth and understanding. This book is my attempt at introducing you, the reader, to the lessons I have learned through the seven days of my mother's *shiva*. I have written my story within the framework of five letters and corresponding postscripts. The letters (acrostically spelling out the word "S.H.I.V.A.") bring you into the house, the heart, and the mind of one who grieves, and the postscripts introduce you to clinical and theological interpretations of the grieving process. Together the two explore the overlap between the teachings of the Jewish Bible and current psychological thought on grief and bereavement.

While the lessons we learn from *shiva* can vary for each of us, one theme resounds throughout: Man "in need" seeks God, and God, through grief, seeks man. Like the "beloved" in Song of Songs who stands at the front of his lover's tent and says, "Open to me" (Songs 5:2), God stands before us, concealed, but never far away. This theme is at the very heart of our journey through *shiva*. Whether we search for solace through expressions of the intellect, or we are guided by hope, faith, emotion or courage, the journey engages our developing spirit. And when we are lost in the midst of a despairing world, it is our spirit that leads us to an encounter with God.

It is my prayer that you find solace, understanding, and perhaps your own connection with God through the words and messages that I have written herein. And for those who have already been, or will one day find yourselves, on a similar path, I pray for your strength and your comfort.

# *Surrender*

Mᴀᴍᴀ,

I write your name and the process begins. *Shiva*: The seven-day period of mourning beginning immediately after your funeral. We are taught that one normally "sits *shiva*" from the moment one returns from the cemetery until after the traditional morning service of prayer six days later. The Sabbath, you have taught us, is deemed so important for communal solidarity that it supersedes the requirements of *shiva*. Thus we really only "sit" for six days, receiving visitors and friends who wish to comfort us, your children, in our beginning hours of pain and sorrow.

As you had explained so many years ago, traditional *shiva* was divided into three time periods: the day of the funeral, the first three days of intense mourning, and the last three days. And it all begins with the "meal of condolence." The meal, usually consisting of basic foods (traditionally a hardboiled egg – an ancient sign of mourning and a reminder of the circularity of life), arrives before we do and is waiting for us upon our return from the funeral. But in our house, the meal of condolence is more lavish and fulsome, as our comforters usher in endless platters of cold cuts and bagels, and trays upon trays of cookies and candy, coffee and tea.

So this is where your story begins, Mom, at the beginning of *shiva* – your seven days of remembrance and honor – as we enter into your house and proceed to mourn, ritually and in accordance with the laws and customs of our faith. Your house, once quiet and comforting, alight with the refracted glow of mirrors and overhead sunlight, is now shrouded in sadness and sheets to cover the mirrors. And we are your cast of characters, your four children – Judi, Robert, Scott and me – our respective life partners and offspring, countless friends and neighbors, our colleagues, relatives and a handful of strangers.

And here I am, ascending the steps of your house alone, ill-prepared for the seven days that are about to wash over me, for I need no ritual plan to guide me through this new land of sorrow. I am accustomed to loving you, near or far, and *shiva* seems sorely able to help me commune with my memories of you. Apprehensive, I wash my hands of the soil from your grave, and climb the lofty stairs, ready to receive the well-meaning words of friends and family. My heart simplified, numb to this new world, I greet the day you have laid out before me.

A house full of guests is already circling around me, like thieves stealing memories and moments of childhood rapture. Platter upon platter is being delivered, doorbell ringing, children running, strangers staring at your things. Faces I haven't seen in years, names I've long since forgotten, rush before me in search of a smile, a story, a sandwich. And as I rise on these childhood steps, I realize that the process of *shiva*, wisely designed long ago as a ritual of honor and remembrance, has morphed and strangely transformed into a solemn party replete with quiet laughter and overabundant food.

I have taken this walk before. I have climbed these steps to greet a room filled with well-meaning comforters six years ago when Dad died. Unaware at the time of all that was about to unfold, I welcomed even the smallest acts of kindness and consolation. I sat where I was told to sit and I let the rites of *shiva* teach me all they were meant to teach.

But this time it feels different, for now we are honoring you, Mom. *Your* life. And I feel more determined to protect your honor, your name, and your house. It is so early in the process and I already feel myself making hasty decisions and passionate mistakes. And indeed, it doesn't take more than one minute for me to "get started," as you would say. For coming directly toward me, I see a woman carrying a rug in the grasp of her hand: your rug, rolled up like a useless newspaper about to be thrown away.

"What are you doing with my mother's favorite rug?" I ask her.

"I'm moving it. It's in the way," she answers.

"But it's my mother's rug. It belongs in the kitchen," I say. And I take the rug out from her unwelcome hands and carefully, angrily place it back where it has lain for years, by the foot of the refrigerator and in front of your sink.

But soon I hear another friend scream out. "Get rid of that thing! It's slipping and sliding and it's in the way." She says, covering a bagel with cream cheese.

"I don't care," I yell.

"But someone will step on it and get hurt," she responds.

"Then don't step on it," I say. "My mother is in the ground only half an hour and already you are rearranging her kitchen."

And suddenly I realize that all eyes are on me and I am being sized-up, interpreted and pitied all at the same time.

". . . Poor man," they say to themselves. ". . . Just buried his mother. He is not taking this well at all," I hear them surmise.

I turn to you and say, "Can you believe this, Mom? Can you believe the chutzpah of these people?" And I hear you say, "Norman . . . people are people. Leave them be. Don't be so angry."

And so begins your *shiva*, Mom. And I am surprised by it all. Surprised by the noise and the laughter, the food and the frenzy. I am met by many different feelings, anger being the strongest. This is not an emotion I had expected to feel at first. As a psychologist and grief therapist, I anticipated feelings of sadness or despair. But anger has rooted itself within me, and I find myself collecting injustices. I ask myself questions such as, "Who isn't here? Who said something indelicate? Who is laughing? And who is eating before offering any of us their condolences?"

I find a chair: the customary "*shiva* chair." An uncomfortable box made of cardboard that is supposed to represent the discomfort I feel in my heart over losing you. I sit lower than the visitors, a reminder of their ability to stand for me in my time of sorrow. And I am met by the rabbi who fastens a threadbare piece of ribbon onto my left lapel, a symbol of my torn heart as I sit and wait. And I wait. I wait for someone to come to me and ask me about you. I long to talk about you, Mom. I want to tell of your beauty, your generosity of spirit and heart. I need to tell someone about the night I received the call. I find myself craving the question,

"What happened?" "Who found her?" "Where were you when you heard the news?"

But no one comes. The house abounds with clamor, with the noise of grief and confusion. Hungry stomachs and broken hearts circle feverishly around me: bagels and lox, pastrami and corned beef. Coffee. Two armfuls of coffee. And I close my eyes and think of Friday. The day you died.

When I open my eyes, I see that someone is offering to make me a plate of food. Gratitude has now replaced my anger. It's strange how a small act of kindness moves me. And I begin to talk, to tell my story of you. I find myself talking incessantly about you and I am comforted by the smiles that your story engenders in others. I notice the littlest things in your house and I discover that I have a memory for each of them. Wordlessly, I review my bank of memories as I scan the room for trinkets and objects that brought you joy when you were alive. I see you standing by the breakfront carefully moving a crystal vase until it rests "just so," and brings a smile to your face. I see you place the tiny clocks from your collection on the edge of the piano, carefully turning them so they all line up in the order you most enjoy seeing them. I hear you closing closet doors filled with linen tablecloths and lace napkins that you washed after use for Sabbath dinner. And I am comforted by your presence, for you are here with me on this solemn day. You smile at me as I try in vain to capture the essence of you in words imprisoned by pain.

I think about how strange this ritual of *shiva* is. I sit here waiting to receive friends and family as they fill the room with kind and loving words. But words rarely penetrate the heart of the griever. Like balm or salve they more likely heal the wounds of the comforter, not the one who needs comforting. For us, the mourners, there are few words. Silence seems better.

And in my silence I find myself disappearing in my mind into the upstairs rooms where no one can find me, or quietly taking a walk around the block, allowing the bounty of your sweet memory to wash over me. In my mind I touch the things you touched when I was young and you were full of life. I peak into your bedside drawer and look through the birthday cards and letters you saved from my days at summer-camp, yellowed from time and tears. I rummage through the downstairs closet and secretly try on old gloves, hats and scarves, misshapen and long since out of style. I sway in the backyard hammock and await your call for dinner, and I pretend not to hear you as I soak up the day's last rays of sun. "Dinner can wait," I hear myself say. You'll always save some food for me.

I see and smell and feel all of these things in my mind and body, though I still remain seated upon this box, and I try to recognize the gifts that the *shiva* process brings. I understand that we are forced to be among friends and family, to be reminded that we are not alone, especially now, in our earliest moments of sorrow. I understand that we are not here for food or drink, that we are meant to be distracted by stories and laughter, compassion and care. And at times I am grateful for this lavish tribute to you, and for these visitors who break my silence and solitude. But at other times I just sit here, overwhelmed and confused.

Here comes your friend, Mom: The one who yelled at me for putting your rug back in the kitchen. She reaches down to me, covering me with one shoulder, and says that she forgives me, for she "knows this is a difficult, horrible day" for me. And she asks me if I forgive her as well. I look in her eyes and I hear your voice telling me to "be nice." I acquiesce, and I accept her apology and, in turn offer my apologies for good measure.

Did I do good, Mom? Did I do the right thing? It took a lot of strength and grit, but as I stand here looking into her eyes, I remember that it is important to honor your name, and that it is my charge to perform the good deeds that you can no longer perform. As I ask her for forgiveness, I pray that she walks away and says, "Selma raised a good son. She taught him well." And so begins the first of many tasks and deeds that I will do as every day I bless you.

It is time for dinner. I turn and see your glass dining room table covered with food, so much food I can't see the lace tablecloth you ached so hard to keep clean. Someone is gently ushering the guests into another room so that we, the mourners, can eat in peace and silence. You would love the display, Mom. It is a veritable confection of everything you were never allowed to eat. There is pickled herring, tongue and roast beef, corned beef, pastrami and brisket, candy coated nuts, towers of chocolate covered fruit set in a picturesque floral display, minted chocolate lentils and fudge, boxes and boxes of bakery goods, Mandel bread and Philly Fluff loaf.

And as I sit to eat, I think to myself, "Who needs such abundance?"

But I look around the silent table and I realize that we need it, Mom. We need the food – all of it – all of the surplus, excess, sugar-coated dedication and love, because we are here at your table without you. And food, as you had taught us long ago, stood for nurturance as well as nutrients. It was your way of loving us. And so I sit at your table and I eat. I eat what I can and I relish the smells and the bounty of the rest. For I know that soon, your house will again be filled with the sounds of well-meaning comforters. And I will once again find myself sitting atop that low-rising box. And as I sit, I will hear you lovingly whisper in my ear, "Did you eat?"

"Yes, Mom. I ate. Oh boy, did I eat."

A strange emotion comes over me as the house begins to fill. People seem to be coming from all over the county on this first night of your *shiva*. Many of Judi's friends are here: some of whom I remember hearing you talk about, others you never met. There are friends here who came for Scott, and they listen to him affectionately in a quiet corner of the upstairs den. Many of your friends are here, some are still married and a few are widowed, and they talk amongst themselves. Robert has visitors from work. And many of my friends have come. I find myself noticing how we, your children, have all taken up separate quarters of your house. We are grieving separately and apart. And I suddenly realize how life has moved us all, and how we find ourselves in different worlds.

Suddenly I see how you kept us all together. Like a harbor standing still in moving waters, you provided a place for us to reunite, to reconvene from our separate worlds and to share with one another.

"So who will be our harbor now, Mom?" I hear myself ask. "Who will keep us together now that our boats seek different and distant waters?"

And I realize that it is our charge, our turn, to keep the family together. And once again, I find myself reminiscing about the past, searching for memories that will keep your harbor strong.

I see you there on the steps between the kitchen and my bedroom, showing me with joy the mittens you bought for me. "How many reindeer do you see?" I hear you say. "Let's count the snowflakes." And I feel the overwhelming love you have for me as I smile and giggle and thank you for the littlest things you give me. Cupcakes with chocolate icing, apricot pie, Starburst candies, and hot wheels cars. Like a shroud you envelop me, your memory protects and nourishes.

I flash forward in time and I see you standing beneath the canopy on my wedding day. I hear you laugh as you incredulously carry the train from Beth's wedding gown and follow her seven times as she circles around me. You didn't warm up to Beth when you first met her, and when I demanded an answer as to why, I cried as I silently realized that it was because you were afraid you were losing me. You did not know at the time the bounty of love and joy that was about to wash over you.

I see you holding Joshua, my firstborn. Your eyes alight with relief: finally a grandson with our last name. I see you smile with hope and promise and salvation. I smell the smells in your kitchen as your tongue tastes his cream of wheat and you add a splash of milk, a dash of salt, and a cache of love.

I see you with your arms outstretched, face aglow with patient anticipation of a kiss that would rarely come from Jacob, my second son. I see you grab him and enfold him in your long, loving arms and you sweep him up and pat him on the behind and try in vain to run your fingers through his long, unruly hair.

I see you standing there in the delivery room as my third son is being born. I remember how you said, "I'll just stand in the corner . . . you won't even know I'm there." And then once in that room, I remember how you stood right in front and blocked the doctor as Davey crowned, and came to this world to bless our family.

I see all of these things from this *shiva* chair where I sit. I see and I feel and I resolve to keep your harbor safe and sound. Like a prisoner, I prowl about the memories of my past, trying vainly to tear down the doors that open to my sibling's separate lives. I realize that this will not be an easy task. But I will try.

Suddenly I feel a tug at my shoulder. It's a friend I have not seen in a long time, and she's here to pay her respects. She leans into my ear and whispers, "How are you?"

It's funny. I'm still trying to find the right answer to that question.

How am I, Mom? You're gone, at least from the world as we know it, and I am supposed to offer a requisite answer to the question, "How are you?" I've tried many answers. My first was a stoic, "As good as expected." But that seemed too generous and kind. I've considered "Ok for now." That one seems to satisfy many. I've even considered, "I don't know." But this answer usually leaves comforters quiet and unsure of what to say next.

But for this distant friend, I lean over and loudly offer a daring, "I'm not good."

And you'll never believe her answer, Mom. She stands straight up and, with a face full of shock and worry, she asks, "Why? What happened?"

Incredulously, I sit there. "My mother is dead," I answer wryly.

And her reply, not unkindly, is, "I know that. But did something else happen?"

So this is how your first day and night of *shiva* has been, Mom: moments of sorrow and disbelief, followed by moments of laughter and insanity. And through all of them, I feel you here with me. I hear you talk to me, telling me to "be nice" to your friends.

I look around and I see many new faces. Some are sullen, others sad. Then I see some distant relatives in the corner. But I see anger, not sadness on their faces. I approach them as they stand and attempt to leave and I say, "I'm so sorry, it's been a long and hard night and I realize I never spoke to you."

"No one has spoken to us, Norman. We've been sitting here for almost an hour and no one has approached us. Where are your brothers? Your sister? I would expect this from other children. But not from any of you."

Here comes the other side of *shiva*, I tell myself, the side that is removed from custom or ritual. This is the side where social politics and religion collide. And once again I think of you and how you deserve to be remembered as a good mother, a woman of valor who taught her children well. So I escort the relatives outside and to their car. One of them can hardly stand anymore, so we walk slowly. And as we walk, they ask me about the night you died. I tell them how Judi found you lying on the floor in my old bedroom. I tell them that you felt no pain and that you asked for a glass of orange juice. I tell them how you didn't want the ambulances, the medics or the doctors. I reassure them that you appreciated their friendship, and I tell them that you were pleased to see their names on the caller ID on your phone just one week ago. And I see in their faces that they are happy, and relieved to learn that they were important to you. I hug them and put them into their car. I promise to call and send the annual holiday picture at Hanukah. And I walk back into your crowded house and proudly tell the others about my last half hour.

But then I hear you whisper in my ear: "You should have let them leave. I stopped calling them years ago for that very reason."

And I laugh because I realize that you and I are different. You remind me to do right by others. But at seventy-nine years of age, you resolved to do and to say whatever was on your mind.

"I've lived long enough," you would explain. "I've earned the right to say what I feel."

This doesn't take away from your elegance, Mom. It makes you more real – for you were a beautiful contradiction – at once loving and painfully honest. You were a measure of goodness and truth. You inhabited the sweet things that surrounded me and you soothed me through the bitterer, more painful parts of my life. And now, your signals keep me on the right path. And your cool critiques … well they guide me too. And I thank you for all of them.

It is now eight o'clock and I realize that it is time for the evening prayers. The rabbi is here from your synagogue. He has come with his *minyan* of ten men, his prayer books and his yarmulkes. Respectfully we climb your stairs to the second floor as the rabbi hurriedly searches for all four of your children.

"They're here," I assure him. "Everyone is here."

But he rushes and doesn't listen to me. He walks around the second level of your house like a landlord evaluating the property. Thankfully Scott, Robert and Judi appear, and we congregate into a mass of quiet dedication. Fifty or more of your friends and relatives are standing at attention, repeating the prayers that are designed to protect your soul and guide it as you make your way up to heaven.

I look around and see one of my friends. He is clearly a stranger in this mass of Jewish prayer and supplication. I turn back and follow along with the prayers the rabbi is reading. I watch as my three children gaze into the distance, unaware of the rituals and practices that they will soon need to learn. I read along with Beth as she struggles to see the ancient Aramaic words through her tears. And I think of my friend standing in the back of the room, a witness to the faith that binds our family together.

Gradually the house begins to quiet down as people start to take their leave. Some I know I will see tomorrow and the remaining days thereafter. Some I realize I will never see again. Since Dad died six years ago, your friends and relatives seem sadly aware that this house, with all of its weight and light, will now have to be taken apart and sold. And I see in their eyes that, for many, this will be their last time standing here. A strange compassion comes over me as I say goodbye to many of them. Their names and faces were the backdrop of my childhood stage. It is nice to see them all again. How sad to know that, for most, this time is the last.

Suddenly I discover that the chatter and noise and laughter around me have dimmed to a low murmur. The remaining comforters and friends are wrapped in deep conversation with one another. And I, myself, am lost in a reverie of stories about you. I am sitting with my friends and colleagues and I am struck by how soothing this last hour of your first day of *shiva* has become. I laugh as I retell the stories of this long day and my friends laugh, too, with understanding and appreciation. Tears come to me as well, and I carefully retrace the steps that brought me to this place. The compassion of my friends covers me and I am filled with gratitude. I am aware of the hard lessons you taught me all those years ago and I am finally being able to utilize them. I appreciate the early mornings and the late nights and the fights and tantrums. I understand the "no's" and I am grateful for the many "yes's" to which you acquiesced. I value the life you tried so hard to create for me and I tell myself that you were right all along. You've done your job, and you've done it well.

I turn my head and I see the last few friends who have yet to say their goodbyes. I feel bad that, as mourners, we are tired and weary from the battle we are being asked to fight. And now I see a kitchen filled with dishes and empty cake boxes, candy wrappers and tin foil strewn about.

My children have left their mark on this "*shiva* party" as well, as I am told that there is a basement filled with toys that need to be put away.

But I am comforted in this last moment of quiet compassion. I find that the remaining visitors truly appreciate the meaning of this day, and I am reluctant to let them go. Sadly I escort my friends to your door and I say my goodbyes. And as I do, I find myself thinking about the contradictions in life. I think about how we are at once afraid of connection, and so desiring of love at the very same time. I think about how life surprises us with moments of unanticipated joy, and how it challenges us with moments of unexpected pain. I revel in the grandeur of it all and I am diminished by the grief. I laugh one moment and I cry the next. And I give in to the contradictions: I surrender to the rush of feelings that wash over me. For I realize at the end of this first day of *shiva*, that all I can manage to do is surrender.

## Postscript

WHAT CAN BE said about the meaning of surrender, and what role does it play in recovery from our pain and despair? As mourners we learn that suffering is an inevitable part of our existence: It is not incidental, nor is it temporary or transient. Pain, we learn through our long days of *shiva*, is a part of the human condition, and its effects linger, consciously or unconsciously, until they redefine the world we once thought of as safe and orderly. Different religions have grappled with the role that suffering plays in the transcendence of the soul. Literature and art have long explored the redemptive and healing components of human despair and the lessons that can be learned through tragedy. And psychology, as well as the Torah, recognizes that sorrow is intertwined in our everyday existence. But what can the concept of surrender teach us about regaining strength, fortitude, and the will to "move on"? In essence we may ask: Is there power in surrender?

Existential philosophers, such as Kant and Nietzsche, as well as Jewish scripture and Jewish thought, all suggest that the answer is yes – there is indeed power in surrender. More specifically, existential and Jewish thought infer that surrender involves transcending the "conceptual continuum," taking a leap of faith and trusting in a universe that contains ultimate goodness and order, even in the face of obvious danger. This gesture of surrender exceeds the boundaries of our usual and everyday thinking styles because it forces us to consider the themes of eternity, infinity, or what the Jewish religion refers to as "*Olam Haba,*" the World to Come. Surrender from this point of view, then, involves deep faith that stands in stark contrast to a belief in a purely sensible and scientifically explainable universe.

A gesture as courageous as this one, however, is often too difficult for the non-spiritual among us. For the spiritually ambivalent or scientifically-oriented man, suffering is more like a dreadful opponent, a "grim reaper," the taker of all things once good and beautiful. Indeed, many of us find ourselves in this category – steeped more in carnal, rather than spiritual experiences. We wake each morning and prepare lunch for our children, we pay the overdue bills, race against time and traffic, and lose ourselves in the stressful tasks of living. Yet when darkness falls, and we are confronted by death, we are ill-prepared to cast off our opinion that the power of evil is more than the power of good. Despair and bewilderment, shock and anger become the internal reflections of our brush with mortality, and we find ourselves struggling for control and meaning. As one mourner stated:

> If there really is a God or great deity, when I die and go to heaven I'm going to have a long talk with Him. First I want to punch His lights out and then I want to ask Him why he took my mother at such a young age. God hasn't met my wrath yet.

Indeed, when we are confronted with the question of suffering, the scientific thinkers among us do not surrender. Technologically-minded, and grounded in the "here and now," some of us find it hard to accept the ontological argument that God has provided a stage for human destiny which is broader than our cognitive reach. Instead, we attempt in vain to conquer evil, we commit to becoming heroes, and we search for triumph over adversity. But these attempts are stillborn from their inception.

Mystery abounds for most mourners, and those who suffer know that some enemies cannot be beaten. The journey for most of us thus begins with a fight against our fate. We beseech help from above and we feel we have been refused. We are angry and we protest, asserting that there is no God, for "No God would ever let this happen to us." And through our suffering, and our unanswered questions, we are forced to face the paradox of our human existence: We are born, we grow, and we move forward in an attempt to understand and conquer nature, only to retreat humbly and face defeat.

This interaction of conflicting forces, this "dialectical movement," as Rabbi Joseph Soloveitchik, known by his students as "the Rav," has called it, is at the very heart of our suffering. The Rav asserts that at every level of human experience, whether it is physical, intellectual or emotional, we must engage in the pendulous movement of "surging forward and swinging back." The search to improve our human condition, to better ourselves and our families, is indeed the prime task with which we have been charged. But adversity and trauma inevitably stand in the way of some of our victories, and we are left feeling lost and uncertain of our next move. Angry and despairing, we are left with two choices: to fight vainly against our fate, denying truth and convincing ourselves that "everything will be alright," or to surrender heroically to our defeat, with the hope of discovering the spiritual wealth that our sorrow has to offer. For the Rav, it is the act of heroic surrender to defeat that brings us closer to our consolation.

Defined in this way, surrender is not an act of *giving up*, rather it is an act of *giving over*. It is an attempt at supplication and submission. Through surrender we renounce our desire for a complete understanding of the order of this world. We concede to being weak sometimes, and we confess to our frailty and helplessness. Surrender is a sacrificial decision in which we, as mourners, lost in darkness, submit to a greater force or a higher decree. We acknowledge that our existence – and all that surrounds it – are the work of a Divine entity. Through this catharsis, this prayerful acknowledgement, we actually experience dignity, even triumph, because we begin to believe in God.

Like Jonah, alone in the belly of darkness, we initially say, "O Lord, take my life from me, I beseech thee, for it is better for me to die than to live," (Jonah 4:3). But God has a different plan for us, for out of silence a still small voice is heard. In our hours of darkness we look heavenward, and we consecrate defeat, raising it to the level of prayer. We recognize that we have no choice but to sit and face the existential terror that comes with being alone. And as we sit and pray, we learn that we are really never alone. For in darkness there is discovery, there is the deciphering of a greater message, and ultimately, there is redemption.

Thus we learn that suffering is a primary medium through which man encounters God: When we are in need, we seek our Creator. Lost and alone we reach out and await a reply. But *shiva* teaches us that suffering is also the channel through which God addresses man. Instead of answering our questions, or telling us the secrets of His creation, however, God demands of us unlimited discipline and absolute submission. We are in a humble position, sitting low on our *shiva* stool, and we bow, ready to receive His decree as well as our salvation. As the Rav, quoting Rabbi Shimon Bar Yochai, one of the noted scholars of the Mishnah, states:

> The Holy One ... gave three gifts to Israel, and He gave all of them only through suffering. They are: Torah, the Land of Israel, and the World to Come.

Indeed, it was through a night of despair and fear that God appeared to Jacob in a dream, a burning bush that God revealed Himself to Moses, and in exile under a "great cloud" that Ezekiel saw visions of God (Ezekiel 1:1). In addition, it was out of a tempest, a fatal whirlwind, that Job heard the voice of his Maker, and learned of His promise of redemption in the World to Come. Sorrow, we discover, delivers its message and, as grievers, we are forced to submit to it so that we may learn what it came here to teach us. In the words of one mourner:

> When I surrender, I allow all of my feelings to come in and wash over me. I welcome the days and the moments when I

cannot function, for I know that in all of this aloneness I will eventually learn how to survive. I also welcome the days I feel my life is sweet, though these days come less often. While there is simply no way that I can make sense of all this pain, I am depending on my belief in something greater, some force or power that will protect me, and help me reach a place of acceptance.

Surrendering thus challenges us to believe in a Divine Being or mystical force that will bring solace and comfort through redemption and growth. As we read in Psalm 23:

> Though I walk in the valley of the shadow of death, I fear no harm, for You are at my side.

This revelation, this catharsis and confrontation with God, ultimately serves to elevate our soul. It teaches us that we are part of a grander fabric whose spiritual reach is farther than our cognitive breadth. We discover that all of our deeds, no matter how small or incomplete, are consummated through God. And we learn that we must have faith, for, in the words of the Sufi poet Jelaluddin Rumi, pain bears its own cure. It cleanses our hearts and challenges our minds. Our questioning never ceases, and through our questioning, self-expansion and dominion prevail over our trauma and sadness.

Unfortunately, for many of us, surrendering, as defined here, is not an easy task to accomplish. In the midst of our mourning, many of us lack the strength or the will to look beyond our current point of view, no matter how hopeful or spiritual we may be. Brokenhearted and confused, some may even find the notion of surrender to be too frightening. In the words of one bereft daughter:

> I don't want to achieve any higher spiritual plane. I don't want to learn the lessons that my mother's death is trying to teach me. I'm afraid to find out who I will be at the end of all of this. Will I still miss her? I'd rather stay sad and feel what I feel. My sadness keeps me closer to her.

Indeed, as human beings, we know we have an ability to determine the kind of emotional life we want to live. We have actions and feelings at our disposal. Emotions can be disowned, rejected or denied; or they can be explored, examined and integrated into our personality. And during times of sorrow, all emotions are noble, even those that protest against the iniquities and injustices of the world. Human suffering cannot be suppressed, nor can it be rationalized or theologized away. Despair, isolation, anger and confusion are all normal and expected parts of the human response to pain. Submission to a "higher will" cannot be achieved without deep questioning, doubt or even disbelief.

Thus, Jewish Law distinguishes between two phases in the process of mourning. We enter into the first phase, called *aninut*, immediately upon the death of a loved one, and we end this phase with the act of burial. Whether taken as a literal directive, or simply as metaphor, this first phase of our grief recognizes that our initial response to death is marked by shock, confusion, and even malice and ridicule toward humanity. "How can life have any meaning if we all must face the same cruel end?" we ask ourselves. "Why carry this moral load if all we are left with is so much pain?" As mourners during this phase of grief, we are exempt from all positive commandments of the Torah. We are even relieved of the requirement to say prayers. It is as if the Torah is saying,

> In the midst of your doubt and despair, you are not expected
> to be capable of spiritual benediction and surrender.

The second phase in the process of our mourning is called *avelut*, and it begins at the time of burial and continues for seven days (the ritual of *shiva*). Thereafter, *avelut* for the death of most relatives lasts thirty days, (called *sheloshim*), and twelve months when we mourn the death of a parent. With the commencement of *avelut*, Jewish law commands us, the mourner, to undertake the valorous task of restoring meaning, dignity and will back into our daily life. It is as if the wisdom of the Sages is teaching us:

> Now is the time to display your greatness – to plant, even
> though you may not be able to eat what you sow; to develop,
> not necessarily for yourself, but for the next generation.

This sentiment is similar to one expressed by the Israeli poet Yehuda Amichai when he said:

> To live is to build a ship and a harbor at the same time, and to continue building the harbor, long after the ship has sunk.

From the poet's prophetic words, as well as from the lessons of religion, we learn that mourning does not remain a physical experience. Rather, it transcends the self and asks us to identify with a timeless future and with the greater world in which we live. Whether accepted as a religious dictate, or understood as a metaphor for the power of the passage of time, Judaism teaches us that a turning point exists in the grieving process. Our initial experiences of shock, self-doubt and despair can and must transform into feelings of determination, self-affirmation and hope. Malice and self-loathing must eventually be replaced with meaning and moral consciousness. As it is said in *Kohelet*, "The day is short and the workload is heavy." But through questioning and protest, our commitment to ourselves and to the world resumes once more.

When does this turning point occur? And what are the catalysts that can help this transformation take place? These are questions whose answers elude us, for we know that grief is not a linear process. It comes and goes in cycles. Like the seasons, or the pull of the tide, our feelings of despair lead us to moments of renewal, only to guide us back into waves of darkness once again. Some of us mourn in solitude, finding great difficulty sharing our pain with well-meaning friends. Others search for fellow mourners who we think will understand sadness as we do. Regardless of our approach, we eventually discover that healing is an interpersonal venture, and it often requires the empathy and compassion of a loving, if not more experienced, listener.

Moses Maimonides, the great Jewish philosopher and physician of the Middle Ages, suggested this idea when he emphasized the notion of "worship of the heart" (in Hebrew, "*Avodah she'baLev*"). According to Maimonides, religious and moral actions must always be endowed with compassion and understanding. In essence, the act of supplication, and service to God and to fellow man, can only be achieved with empathy and love. This is also true during times of sorrow. Healing, like prayer, requires love and understanding.

The archetype for this definition of healing can be found through the ancient ceremony of *Parah Adumah*, the burning of a red heifer and its conversion into ashes and spring water. In biblical times, when a man came into contact with the carcass of a dead animal, he was required to immerse himself in the "living waters" of a stream, river or ocean. This act of cleansing was performed so he could rid himself of "impurity." But when a man came into contact with human death, immersion in "living waters" alone was not sufficient. Rather, the sprinkling of spring water, mixed with the burned ashes of a red heifer, was required for man to regain his status of "purity." Moreover, the process of sprinkling had to be performed by someone else, likely a High Priest, for man was not allowed to sprinkle the mixture of water and ashes upon himself.

The difference between these two ancient acts of ritual cleansing represents a basic tenet of the human condition. In times of sorrow, we have the ability to raise ourselves from the depths of pain and hardship through supplication, self-care and immersion in life-sustaining activity. We go to the gym. We give ourselves breaks from the usual stress of everyday life. Some of us change our eating habits, begin to lose weight and gain energy and self-confidence. But in times of mourning, self-care alone is not enough. We must enjoin the help of another, wiser or more experienced listener: we cannot cleanse our souls alone.

The Gemara, the book of Jewish Oral Law, supports this notion as it records several incidents in which sages were afflicted with suffering and required the help of another. In particular, when Rabbi Yochanan, a rabbi in the era of the Talmud, fell ill, his counterpart Rabbi Chanina went to visit him, asking:

> "Are these afflictions dear to you?"
> Rabbi Yochanan answered, "Neither they nor their reward."
> Rabbi Chanina then said to him: "Give me your hand," and Rabbi Chanina revived him.
> The Gemara asks, "Why did Rabbi Yochanan need another rabbi's help? Why couldn't he revive himself?"

And the Gemara answers, "A captive cannot release himself from prison. He needs help from someone outside." (Bavli *Berachos* 5b)

Thus, Jewish faith teaches us that we, as mourners, need the strength and compassion of someone else to redeem us from the impurity of our darkness. Moreover, the help of another must contain two competing but necessary elements: The listener must acknowledge our confrontation with death (the impurity), while recognizing our need to continue on with our lives (the living waters.) Without this help, this loving attention, we cannot be freed from our suffering, and a "turning point" will not occur. In the words of one mourner:

> My grief feels to me like a bottomless pit: There is always more of it waiting to be released, and I feel as if I have no control over it. I am always trying to prevent a dam from breaking which would cause uncontrollable grief to be spewed everywhere. And that is why grief therapy is such a respite for me: It is the only place, other than in my home, where I really don't care if the dam breaks. And that is helpful because keeping the dam from breaking is exhausting. And now that I think of it, I suspect this is why I don't have a desire to see many other people, even caring people, because when I am with them, I feel forced to expend so much energy just trying to keep the damn dam from rupturing. It therefore does not surprise me that I find myself withdrawing from the world and living week to week, until my next therapy appointment, or staying close to the one or two friends who truly understand how I feel.

Thus, whether we understand the ancient ritual of the burning of the red heifer as religious law, or interpret it as a metaphor for the healing power of human love and connection, the outcome remains the same: When we surrender, and we ask for help from another, a turning point in our grief occurs. We are not like Adam who hid in the Garden of Eden and said:

> I heard your voice God and I was afraid. I hid myself. (Genesis
> 3:9–10)

Rather, we reach outward and upward for help and support, and we discover new ways of mastering our pain and sorrow. We learn that other mourners have felt similar to the way we are feeling now, and we see how others made it through their long nights of darkness. This outreach ultimately helps us to develop ways to achieve self-expansion, outward growth and inner peace. Our charge is to learn how to wrestle with our sorrow, to revisit and embrace, even befriend, what is most frightening inside of us. In the words of the poet Rainer Maria Rilke, perhaps everything terrible is in its deepest being something that wants help from us.

Thus, through surrender, and through our connection with a healthy and loving other, our commitment to ourselves and to God will prevail. We are being asked to turn to others in our time of sorrow. But we are also being asked to turn inward toward our highest selves, and to our deepest faith, to uncover who we are and what we hold most sacred. We are ending the phase of *aninut*, where confusion and despair once ruled; and are now beginning the period of *avelut*, where meaning and dignity are meant to be restored. And if we are successful in our challenge, we will discover that, unlike the waves of pain that once pulled us under, surrender will buoy us. It will lift us through the mist of our tears, to a place where self-awareness and self-growth can flourish. There are indeed times when we may still see the world through a haze of sadness and confusion, but our future, and God's place in it, comes more clearly into view.

# The Five Letters of *Shiva*

# *Hope*

Dᴇᴀʀ Mᴏᴍ,

It is the second day of *shiva* and I rise to meet the morning. What lessons do you have for me to learn today? Whom will I meet and who will teach me something new about you: something different or secretive, sensual or serene? I awaken to the sounds of distant noise in my head. Words and sounds and laughter circle around my mind as I recount the rush of attention we all received at your house yesterday.

It is six-thirty in the morning and I have to get ready quickly for the morning prayers. I shower, dress and kiss Beth and the boys. Then off I run to the synagogue where you used to pray. It is a twenty-minute drive and I hope I make it there on time.

"Don't be late," I hear you beckon. "I should have told you the services started at six. This way you'd be there on time."

I drive in silence and I listen to your words as you chide me and laugh at my flaws.

"What do you want from me, Mom?" I ask. "I've got a wife, three sons, two jobs, a mortgage to pay. I'm doing the best that I can." This was my standard answer to your ever-present reminders of my poor timeliness.

I make it to synagogue at seven-fifteen. Fifteen minutes late. And as I stand there opening my *tefillin*, the two small leather boxes containing texts from the Hebrew Scriptures, and I ritually wrap the straps of one box around my arm seven times, I see a man I barely recognize. Face old and weathered, he turns to me and asks:

"Your mother had a doctor?"

"What?" I ask blindly.

"Did your mother have a doctor?" he repeats. "A hospital? Was she in the hospital?"

"Yes," I answer as I continue vainly to concentrate on the seven circles of leather that lie hopelessly around my left forearm.

"It was the doctors that killed her, you know. They kill 'em all." He continues. Then he says, "Hospitals . . . . not for me. No way, no how . . . . Haven't been to a doctor in sixty years . . . and look at me."

And indeed I do. I raise my head up from my prayer book and, looking straight ahead into the eyes of the old man, I realize that the second day of your *shiva* has indeed begun.

★

I go home after morning services, but on the way I stop in front of your house and suddenly I see the gardener mowing your lawn. For forty-six years he mowed that lawn. And as he did, he watched as our family grew. We were four little children running about on his freshly cut grass, aging, growing and leaving home.

"You're one of the twins," he says to me. "I remember you when you were this high." And he places his hand close to the newly cut grass.

"Yes, I'm one of the twins, Selma's third child."

"And how is your mother? I haven't seen her in a while. Is she on a vacation?" he asks me.

And suddenly I realize that I have to tell him the news of your death. He is unprepared to hear the words I have rehearsed and found myself saying day after day to countless neighbors and friends.

"My mother, I'm sad to say, has died."

Silently he stood there, witness to the changing calendar of my life, and said, "Oh my God. This is not the news I wanted to hear today." And he cried.

How many more hearts am I going to have to break today? I ask myself. How many more people will I run into that you have touched and left? And with a heavy heart, I get into my car. I watch him stand at attention in front of your house, the house he tended for so many years. And I drive away.

It is eight-thirty when I arrive back home and I find that everyone is still asleep. I climb the stairs and quietly enter into my boys' bedrooms, and I watch them as they lie in morning slumber, and I think of the day I had to tell them that you died. I remember how I lied at first and said that you were sick and in the hospital.

"Awareness comes slowly," I told myself. "Like honey dripping from a spoon." I remind myself that children do not integrate trauma into memory in the same way that adults do. Your death was too sudden and unexpected for any of us to accept, so I decided to introduce them to the sad news gently, and with considered warning.

I took them to a park and let them run around for a long while. Eventually, I called all three of them together. We arranged ourselves in a circle, Beth to my right, and the boys all around us. I told them how you had been taken to the hospital last night. I told them how you were feeling weak and the doctors wanted to check on you. I reminded them of how late we came home after visiting you and that you were not doing very well.

"Her heart?" Joshua said. "Did Grandma have another heart attack?" he asked.

"Yes, Josh. Grandma had another heart attack. And she got weaker because of it: so weak that it became hard for her to breathe."

Looking around at the circle Beth and I had created, I realized that this is one of the moments in a life that isn't easily forgotten. I think about how in one short instant, all three of them will have a new view of the world; how they will have different feelings about the safety of any of us.

"Well," I continue, "Grandma's heart got very tired. It became harder and harder for it to keep ticking. And finally, it stopped. And she died."

What happened next was a surprise. Jacob, at seven, came over to me and, hugging me close, he said "Don't worry, Dad. I'm always gonna remember her. You can be happy now because Grandma's soul went up to heaven to be with Grandpa."

Little Davey, you'll be charmed to learn, didn't quite understand the news. At age five, he sees death only as a state of separation. So he took his lead from Jacob, and as Jacob began to cry, so did Davey. He cried tears of allegiance and compassion for an older brother whom he adores.

And then he turned to me and said, "I know that Grandma went to heaven, Daddy. But don't worry. She'll be back soon."

Joshua had the hardest time with the news. At age eight, he understood the permanence of death. He was the closest to you of the three boys, having spent many years by your side as you prepared the holiday meals, washing the vegetables and peeling potatoes, telling stories and listening closely to us adults as we worried about you.

He cried loudly, breaking the silence that surrounded us. And as I tried to comfort him I realized that these were the first of many tears he will shed for you. And as he cried, I found myself thinking about the precariousness of life. I thought about how one day, without warning, a telephone rings, a doctor enters a consulting room, or a newspaper headline calls out. I thought about children and about how quickly the people they are at one moment can be changed forever in the next.

But that is the way it is, Mom. You teach us in death like you taught us in life, for we have much pain to endure and many lessons yet to learn. I try to carry on with the teaching of your lessons. And everyone reminds me that now it is my turn to bear the weight of the years gone by.

Eventually, I make my way to your house to greet the second day of comforters, mourners and friends. Your house is slowly filling with people. It is quieter than I had expected, though it is still early, and I make a pledge to be "be good" like you always asked. I decide to sit quietly on my low *shiva* box and listen as people pass by. And I search for hope.

The daughter of one of your best friends is here. You'd be happy to learn that she is as beautiful as you remembered her. I make my way over to where she is sitting and thank her for coming. And she says that she would not have missed the chance to honor you. She tells me that she'll never forget how wonderful you were to her when her own mother died.

I smile as she tells me stories of you and her mother stealing cigarettes and smoking them in the bathroom on the vacations you used to take. And I revel in the belief that the two of you are together again, somewhere in a state of laughter, maybe even stealing a cigarette or two for good measure.

These are the times when I find the *shiva* process to be pleasant and soothing. The sun is shining and only a handful of your friends and relatives are here, and I am learning new and sweet things about you. I laugh and cry comfortably knowing that I am in good company. I sort through old pictures and I feel grateful for the uncovering of memories that were lost or hidden. But I know this moment will be brief, for soon enough this house will be filled with the distraction of many people I hardly even know.

I am learning many things about the process of early grief. I recognize that I am still in a suspended state of shock, for you have only been gone three days. I am discovering how the movement of time eludes me. I am losing all references to milestones and "age markers." Birthdays and holidays have taken on a new meaning now, and I realize that this week of *shiva*, with its love and distraction, has left me frozen in time. It is as if everything moves on around me while I sit here on top of this *shiva* box, trapped in memory and loss. Yet for others, deadlines still need to be met, mortgages must be paid. Even the expiration date on the milk is approaching.

I discover how this exercise in attention and compassion forces me to haul up my deepest sorrow in the presence of people I never thought I would see again. I am grateful to have an audience to whom I can tell my story: my story of you. And I am introduced to a host of emotions I thought I put away years ago: fear, panic and anger.

I am learning that the very act of living indisposes us to death. Unless confronted with loss or tragedy, most of us go about our days gloriously unaware and fiendishly grateful that the tragedies we hear about are happening to someone else, somewhere else. I find myself wondering if this process will teach me to discover ways to live in this new and emptier world, and I pray that I will one day again speak of strength and hope, as I realize that hope is what I am in search of now.

I am learning to accept the loving overtures of others, for I realize that they ache for you too, especially your neighbors Shoshanna and Henry. You'd be amazed at how much Shoshanna has been cooking. She made us homemade Israeli salad and humus. I know you wouldn't eat any of it. But I am happy to oblige them as I know that, like you, this is their way of showing us their love. I imagine I'll see them here every day, and I am comforted by the feelings of warmth they invoke in me.

There are other people who are becoming "regulars" here but I don't quite know who they are. I have started referring to them, not unkindly, as *The Shiva Sisters*. They are friends with someone in my family, I'm sure, and I feel as if they are unconsciously drawn to the love and connection that this house of mourning evokes in them. They seem to come twice a day, every day, and they sit in the living room, drinking coffee and looking for someone to comfort. Sometimes I see them folding table linens or stuffing the trash into garbage bags and organizing the kitchen. I realize that they mean well. But sometimes their presence makes me uncomfortable.

I decide to go into the backyard. The hammock is still here and the sun is warm and high in the sky. I ask myself, "If I take a nap will I insult anyone? If I run a few miles to release some stress, will anyone know?" With the sounds of *shiva* in my ears, I lie down on my childhood hammock and close my eyes and think of you. Moments of quiet are rare these days. I find myself craving silence: profound oceans of silence. For in silence you come to me. You comfort me and tell me everything is going to be ok:

"It'll all work out just like it's supposed to," I hear you say. And you gently pat me on the cheek and say, "Sleep, *Mamenyu*. Sleep. You'll need the energy for later." And once again I am lost in my memories of you.

I see you standing at the bottom of the stairs with a bag of *challah* bread in your hand. I liked it whole. You liked it sliced. I hear you as you climb the stairs, left leg always first as you learned to do after the hip surgery years ago. I follow you into the kitchen as you drop your keys on the table and instinctively open the refrigerator to feed me. Even if there isn't "a stitch of food in the house," you'll find something for me to eat.

Memories and odors and sounds come rushing through me as I sway gently in the late summer breeze. Like a fugitive I run from the rooms inside your house that remind me of your absence. I lie here and wait for feelings of hope to greet me and assure me that, as you always said, "It'll all work out."

I am awakened by the ring of my cell phone. It is one of my patients, and she is calling me from inside of your house.

"Dr. Fried, we are here but we cannot find you. We came to pay our respects."

"I'm outside in the backyard. I'll be up in a moment." I say, and I am quickly brought back into the present.

Once inside, I am met by three people. The first is a tall man staring at me with a sad look in his eyes. I realize suddenly that it is a patient with whom I work in therapy every Friday morning. His son was killed by a car while roller-skating six years ago this very week, and he is here, today, arms extended in kindness and understanding. Behind him is the patient who called, along with her husband, and they lost a son last year to cancer. I invite them all to sit with me for a while. But I cannot speak. I sit quietly, pressed in silence and dwarfed by the magnitude of their compassion.

My story, the story of your death and of my grief and shock, seems suddenly small beneath the vaulted pain of these three people. I tell myself that this is the way things are supposed to be, that if we live long enough, there will come a time when we must bury our parents. I convince myself that this is the proper order of things, and I think of how fortunate it is that you made it as far as you did.

I begin to tell them about the things I am learning from this ancient ritual of *shiva*. I tell them about the scores of people who have walked through your house in the last two days. I tell them about the crazy things some of them have said to me, and about the kind gestures others have performed. And I see in their eyes that they understand. Veterans of their own battles, my stories make sense to them. I find myself laughing and crying and embracing the love that they offer.

After a while, I realize that it is time for them to leave. I walk them outside to their cars and hug each one of them. I stand there watching as they drive away from your house and I think to myself, how strange the journey through grief. The heartbroken console the heartbroken; we speak a language that only we can understand. As I turn to re-enter your house, I suddenly feel the first wave of hope come over me. I kiss the *mezuzah* on your doorpost and climb your stairs, ready to greet the rest of this second day of your *shiva*.

The evening is descending and I am aware that the crowds, with their attendant cacophony, will soon return. Our neighbors will be here quietly watching over us as you would have done. I expect *The Shiva Sisters* to return for dinner and distraction from their ordinary lives. And I am strangely hopeful to meet the countless others who have yet to pay their respects to you.

Everyone is eating dinner in the kitchen, but I am not hungry. I go upstairs and sit quietly on a chair in your living room and think about all of the things you are teaching me. I think about hope, and how we all search for signs of you. I think about the messages you thought you were getting from Dad years after he died. I smile as I remember the joy you experienced when you would see a flickering light or you would hear a song on the radio that you believed was a gift from him. And I find myself asking you to do the same for me. I ask you for bumper stickers and songs and distant moonlight to guide me through the dark nights ahead. Like a beggar I make this plea, and await your answers. And I convince myself that I will find them. I tell myself that I will learn a new language of symbols so I can stay connected to you.

I look up and see that the rabbi is here. It must be time for the evening prayers. The day is quickly coming to a close. I stand, fasten a skullcap on my head, open a prayer book and pretend to pray. Around me are people, rows and rows of people, all standing in silent dedication to the God that gave you life and took you back.

Suddenly I feel a tug at my leg. It's Josh and he has a question for me.

"Daddy," he proudly asks, "If today's tomorrow was yesterday's tomorrow's today, what day is it?"

Confused and a bit disoriented, I lean down and tell him that we need to be quiet. "The rabbi is in the middle of the evening prayers," I remind him.

But he persists. "No really. This is a good one. Try it," he goads. "If today's tomorrow was yesterday's tomorrow's today, what day is it?"

And I stand there trying to figure it out. I am struck by the paradox of *shiva*. How at once we can be lost in our search for answers to our questions and for signs from above, while at the same time be involved in the beautiful mundane tasks of living.

"Today!" I shout. "Today."

"Right, Daddy. Got me again," he says. And in an instant he is gone, back to the basement from where he came. And I thank him for I realize that today is a day for hope.

After services, your house begins once again to quiet down to a distant low murmur. This, I realize, is my favorite time of the *shiva* day. It is an hour filled with close friends and meaningful conversation. And as I approach my chair I see Shea. I am stunned by his presence. I am both frightened and comforted at the same time. You didn't know his name, Mom, but I certainly did. His name is Shea. Shea Farkas, and he is the medic that found you on the floor as you lay dying upstairs. He is the man who performed the necessary life-saving procedures that kept you living long enough for me to arrive and say goodbye to you. He is also a friend of mine with whom I have sat throughout the years, debriefing with him from the vicarious pain he felt after hours of service to the sick and the dying. And in some stroke of fate or mere coincidence, it was Shea who was called to your side on the night you died.

I ask Shea a host of questions. I want to know if you were conscious when he arrived. I ask him if you were in pain. I ask if you called out any of our names, or if you asked for your mother. I am driven with a need to know everything. I am filled with wonder and worry, curiosity and compassion. Shea gently tries to answer my questions. He is a good man. And in my eyes, he is a noble and holy man. He was with you in the ambulance and he was there at the hospital when I eventually arrived. He stayed with me through the ensuing hour and he cried as he saw the emergency room doctors take their leave from you.

And suddenly I remember. Suddenly I hear his name come from deep within my memory.

"Farkas . . ." I hear you call me. It is morning, forty years ago, and I am asleep in my bed and you call me by the name "Farkas," as you did every morning to wake me. Farkas was your nickname for me as a child.

"Wake up, Farkas," you say. "Wake up and get ready for school."

And now, as I stand before the man who revived you as you lay dying on the floor of my old bedroom, I realize that he has the same name as the nickname you used to call me every morning as a child.

I look up from my chair and I smile, because I know that you are here, living, all about me, laughing and dancing and answering my questions. I tell myself that you have come to me with your signs. Did you know, Mom? Did your soul surmise, all those years ago, that your fate, and all that was to happen after, was scripted, pre-ordained or determined in some ancient Elysian Field of the blessed long before we were all born?

I am confused and amazed and comforted all at the same time, and I find myself not seeking any more answers tonight. I feel you here with me. I feel the rush of hope that I asked you for as it washes over me like a spindrift of fallen tears, and I realize that hope is all I need to make it through the rest of the night.

## *Postscript*

WHAT IS THE meaning of hope, and how can it help us through our days and nights of despair? For many, hope is a quality that imbues us with grace in the face of adversity. It is an internal process that allows us to encounter the world with awe and faith in a more numinous realm, an intrinsic and existential mindset of being. For others, hope is synonymous with "want" or "expectation." It denotes a passive, "wait and see," approach to a desired object or outcome. Understood in this way, hope is a state of mind, a wish or thought born from distress and defeat. But I see hope as a dynamic process involving "active pursuit." Hope compels us to envision our goals, to determine ways to reach those goals, and to employ willpower to see our goals through to fruition. Hope makes us creative. It challenges us to discover strategies for survival through the use of commitment, connection and action. And through this active process, hope engenders faith. It forces us to recognize that we are not alone in this world, and that we must think and act with a higher power in mind.

Psychologists have long studied the formation and growth of hope in infants and children. These studies suggest that an important ingredient of hope is "goal selection," and that this behavior begins to develop immediately after birth. Specifically, every one of us as infants has to learn how to select necessary and life-sustaining goals for ourselves. Through crying we discover ways to receive food, protection and comfort from our mother or caregiver. Through anger or temper tantrums, we learn how to change the way our caregiver treats us. Once these more basic needs are met, we begin to seek further stimulation: We become curious about the larger world around us. We discover that pointing to a toy ends in our receiving that toy, and crying when we are hurt results in receiving succor and support.

As we grow, we employ more abstract reasoning skills, as well as creative strategies, to get what we want. We learn to ask politely rather than to scream or demand for things. We know that a smile can be more effective than a frown in eliciting a hello from a stranger or friend. These more mature skills become the precursor for the next ingredient of hope, namely, determination. Through frustration and "trial and error," we become determined to overcome obstacles that keep us from attaining our goals. And with persistence, as well as reinforcement from those around us, most of us begin to perceive ourselves as capable of effecting change in the world.

But some of us were exposed to extreme stress and trauma at an early age, and we learned to "shut down" or to abandon strategies we once thought were effective and successful. This is how all of us feel when we experience grief and loss. Trauma and bereavement make us question our self-confidence and our sense of effectiveness, as well as our self-worth and our inner pride. Like children who have been over-exposed to stress, those of us who are grieving begin to believe that some goals are simply unattainable. Efforts we once thought of as helpful and promising become elusive. We have stopped strategizing. We lost hope.

Thus, we search for willpower. In their research on infant and child development, authors McDermott and Snyder assert that willpower is the third ingredient of hope. They define willpower as the supply of mental energy and emotional commitment we use to pursue our goals. Willpower requires us to focus, to eat better, to exercise and to use self-care. It demands of us patience and practice. It asks us to identify our negative and self-defeating thoughts and it challenges us to replace them with positive statements and beliefs. Instead of telling ourselves that we "will not survive this loss," or that "we cannot live without our mother in our lives," we assure ourselves that we "will find a way to live again."

The overlap between current psychological theories on hope and ancient writings from the Bible is vast, for Judaism has wrestled with the concept of hope from the beginning of time. Indeed, perhaps the first example of hope in human form was Adam in the Book of Genesis. Like an infant who is forced to learn necessary and life-sustaining goals for himself, Adam was forced to survive the challenges of the new and potentially menacing world into which he was cast. He was given a mandate by God to "fill the earth and subdue it" (Genesis 1:28), to be fruitful and multiply, and to have dominion over every living thing – from beast and fowl to every herb yielding seed. Through this first account of Adam, we learn that all of us are endowed as creative beings. We are fashioned in the "image of God" and we are blessed with great drive and with an ability to be "creators." We have strategies, resources and our intelligence all at our disposal. And through our curiosity and determination, we develop the willpower to conquer, master, and even dominate over our sorrows.

The Rav, the great scholar and authority on the meaning of Jewish law, expounds from this first account of Adam that we, as a people, are interested in the practical and the functional aspects of our world. Like Adam, we ask about how things work. We are born with an attraction as well as a quest to understand the "how" of behavior, and we strive to improve our environment, our health, and our lives. In order to be successful, we need to learn the *ways* of the world, we need to be able to harness the elements around us and put them to good use. Born from this practical need, thus, is our willpower to learn the secrets of nature.

More importantly, the Rav asserts that we struggle to learn the ways of the world, and to triumph over nature because we were created in "the image of God." We are adventurous but obedient, and we are guided by a need for perfection, function and productivity. This interpretation casts Adam, and everyone who grieves, as hopeful individuals whose natural reaction in the face of adversity is to survive through finding solutions and cures, conquering opposition and achieving goals. In the words of one patient:

As I watch my mother, who is afflicted with a rare dementia, linger in a state of suspended reality, where every day is the same day for her, a repetitive existence where her memory and speech and self-awareness are all but lost now, I tell myself that she will get better. I tell myself that there must be something that science can do to help her. Nothing comes. But still I have hope. I search for alternative cures, medicines that are being used in other countries, and I hope I will find a way to make her better.

Like Adam, hope asks us to master our traumas. It compels us to find solutions to the challenges that life has put before us. It demands focus, connection, partnership and action. Most important, hope requires our indomitable spirit, our need for succor, and our wish for knowledge and success.

There appears, however, to be a second account of the creation of Adam in the beginning of Genesis. This second account suggests for me that the man of hope transcends into a man of faith. Faith asks Adam to search for answers that are far beyond his cognitive reach, and it forces him to accept that not all mysteries can be explained. In this second account, Adam is described as having a different approach to the mandate he was given. More specifically, this second Adam is not a man who is interested in *how* things work, but in *why* things exist in the first place. Adam Two was placed in the Garden of Eden with a mandate to "cultivate it and keep it" (ibid., 2:15), and is thus tragically in search of an *understanding* of the world into which he was cast. He encounters his environment with wonder, awe and naïveté. Like those of us who grieve, Adam is alone and alienated from the world, and he turns his focus inward and struggles to find his identity.

Through this second account of Adam, we learn that we are a people who were not only born as "creators," but as "seekers" as well. All of us are, at times, like Adam Two searching for a catharsis, redemption, and a hallowed existence. When we mourn we discover that we are charged, not only with control over our environment, but also with control over ourselves. In times of sorrow we recoil, we reflect and retreat. And in our solitary search for meaning and answers, we discover that we must allow ourselves to be defeated. We come to learn that there are some things we will never truly understand. And when we concede to defeat, we are confronted by a higher power and a greater plan. This confrontation offers us, as Kierkegaard suggests, a chance to gain "infinite reality" by being conscious of existing before God.

This second account of the creation story shows us that we are a people of faith as well as a people of hope. Like Adam Two, there are times when each of us is receptive and curious. When we grieve, we search inward for relief and, when no relief comes, we begin to encounter God. Faith asks us to surrender to distress and defeat. It demands discipline, self-control and a belief in something grander and it promises solace as a reward. In the words of one patient:

> I think of people who have no faith and then I think of the words we read in the *Hallel* service in shul on Rosh Chodesh: "*They have eyes but they can't see, they have ears, but they don't hear, they have noses but do not smell, their feet, they do not walk, the hands do not feel . . .*" But I have faith. And I know that I am more alive on this day than anyone because I seek the world that God lives in. I want to know its walls and ways. It is like paddling but in the opposite form, ever so quiet, so as to hear and see and smell and walk and feel.

Thus, through *shiva* we see that the search for hope begins with the pursuit of a goal – to know the world's *ways* and to learn the secrets of nature – and it ends with faith as we search for the *whys*, leading us to venerate the One who guards all of the answers. Like the infant who craves attachment and independence from its caretaker both at the same time, when we hope, we encounter God with desire and awe, run away, and then look back to assure ourselves that He is still there. Like Moses who hid his face from the burning bush (Exodus 3:6), we run, only to yearn for unity with our Creator later, as when Moses finally longed to see God's face at Mount Sinai (ibid., 33:18). In the words of one patient:

> I never believed in God before. As a child I would run from my mother when it was time to go to prayer service. But now,

as I look at my mother, day after day dying in this hospital bed, I think to myself, "She was right all along. There really must be a God, for I need Him now more than ever."

Hope and faith thus consummate a dual existence in every man. Hope starts us on a path toward understanding and action, and it leads us to a place of wonder and elevation. With hope, we act with dignity and responsibility. We become dynamic and creative, attempting mastery over our world. We ask our doctors for help or we search the internet for answers to medical questions. Some of us raise money to find cures for our loved ones who are ill, while others reach out to legislators and law-makers to effect change in government policies on medical and pharmaceutical endeavors.

But in our searching we discover that we must direct ourselves inward as well. Some of us read through prayer books, and others study with religious leaders and practice God's ways. Still others among us link ourselves to the chain of history that brought us here and, as the Jewish scholar Maimonides said in his *Guide of the Perplexed*, we attempt to "know the knower" like our forefathers and spiritual leaders did generations before.

Indeed, as Maimonides asserts, in our struggle to know our world and ourselves better, we begin to see and honor God's "infinite wisdom and wondrous works." The Torah refers to this transformation as a state of "*devekut*" or "cleaving," for one cannot truly know the ways of the world without knowing and loving the ways of God. Cleaving is an embrace of love and friendship between man and God that is marked by an independence from fear and awe. As the Rav asserts, it is a state of being that unites thought, will and action, endowing us with deeper compassion and a conscious devotion to each other. Cleaving anchors us more firmly in the world. It enables us to give of ourselves more unreservedly because our identity no longer feels endangered. Through cleaving we see God in ourselves; we are not afraid.

This state of cleaving, this embrace between man and God, is no better illustrated than in the story of Vincent, a nineteen-year-old patient who, at the time of my work with him, was dying from an inoperable brain tumor. The third son in a family of four boys born to immigrant Italian parents, Vincent had grown from a once healthy and talented soccer player and artist into a weak and tired young man who lay in the dark of his room reading from his Bible. On days when Vincent was too weak to read out loud, he led me to the passages he wished to hear. And one day, in the midst of my reading, he stopped me and asked:

"Do you believe?"

"Do I believe what, Vincent?"

"Do you believe that God was able to heal the sick?"

I sat quietly for a while, hoping not to interrupt the course of Vincent's prayers.

"I don't know," I finally replied.

And after a long silence, he looked up at me and said, "Please promise me that you will read His words. I believe that God heals the sick, and I want you to believe also."

Hours later, when Vincent died, his mother took me by the hand and guided me to the bed where he lay, saying "I knew that God would perform a miracle. I knew that He would heal my boy. And He has. For now my son is with God. He is finally healed."

The ability to cleave to God thus comes through hope and faith. But as we have seen here, it also comes through knowledge. As we search for hope we must also commit to learning and growing with every new day. We need to study the ways of the world and practice what we learn, perfecting ourselves in relation to our friends and neighbors. Like Vincent, who spent his last days on earth reading and cleaving to God in an act of love and devotion, our search for greater knowledge will eventually allow us to unite with the mysteries of the world that are yet unknown.

Thus, we discover the confluence of two life forces. Hope sets us on a path toward attaining our goals. It helps us determine strategies for living, and it generates in us the willpower to make our goals into a reality. And when all hope seems lost, we turn to our faith, for faith asks us to look inward and to think differently. Faith guides us to develop spiritual pursuits, to achieve victory by accepting defeat. And through both we encounter God's ways and we are challenged to unite with Him. We are indeed rational beings. We have an inherent wish to create a livable world, replete with the hope of grace and dignity. But we are also spiritual beings, we have a need to honor and accept what is unlivable through sacrifice, faith and love. And through an appreciation of both, we know we will heal as we continue on our long journey through grief.

# *Ire*

GOOD MORNING, MOM,

It is the third day of your *shiva* and I rise to greet the morning sun and the lessons you have to teach me today. As is becoming the custom, I quickly dress, kiss Beth and the boys, and make my way, late again, to your synagogue to say the morning prayers. I think about the two days that have just passed, about surrender and hope, and the mystery that surrounds all of us. I think about my children as they play every *shiva* day in your basement, seemingly unaffected by the changes occurring in my heart. I think about your neighbors who are probably preparing another meal for our family at this very moment. I think about the rabbi, and about my siblings and how they must be waiting with the *minyan* of ten men and women for the prayer services to begin.

A beard is beginning to grow on my face. As is customary, I have decided not to shave for the requisite thirty days after your funeral. "*Sheloshim*" it is called. Literally meaning "thirty," these days represent the period of mourning through saying *Kaddish*, the ritual prayer exalting God's virtues. An ancient tradition teaches that Divine judgment for the deceased requires the reciting of a mourner's prayer throughout these thirty days. Although the official period of mourning extends to just under a full year, many mourners say the *Kaddish* for only thirty days.

I drive toward your synagogue and I ask myself, "Do you really want me to get up this early every morning to say these prayers? Do you hear me as I stand before the ark of scrolls that holds the wisdom of our faith? Does your soul, so gentle and beautiful, require my exaltations in order for it to arrive to the holy place from whence it came? And this beard, Mom: I hear you saying to me, "Shave, Norman. I can't stand that dirt on your face."

But still I drive forward, faster and faster, and I think about how time is passing and people are probably waiting. Somehow the ritual of saying the *Kaddish*, a prayer that has been read for centuries before you and I were born, seems to bring me comfort. There is a supportive community in the prayer service where mourners come together and speak a similar language of loss. And contact with these people and their customs brings me closer to you, to your traditions and values.

I arrive just in time to be greeted by the old man who, only yesterday, told me his thoughts on the reasons for your death. I say hello, and with my eyes facing the ground, I hurry into the chapel. Services already underway, I begin to wrap the *tefillin* seven times around my left forearm. I pray for your soul and I pray for moments of peace from the sadness I feel.

When the morning prayers are finished, I start my car and make my way back home. But as I drive, I notice how anger begins to stir within me. I am struck by how quickly my feelings have changed, and I am suddenly overwhelmed with a need for speed and movement. Instead of reaching home, I see the gates of the high school track in our neighborhood, and I park my car. I decide to run the track, to let my thoughts and my feelings carry me wherever they may. I am aware of the insidious nature of ire, how it works its way through us until we are unable to ignore it any longer. I ask myself what it is I am angry about, and I flash back in time to the night we returned home from the hospital. I remember how the four of us, your children, walked into your house and called out your name.

"Ma!!!" we screamed, half-expecting to find you sound asleep in your bed upstairs. I wanted to hear you say, with that brush of annoyance in your voice, "What do you want? I'm here sleeping. Close the front door."

But we were greeted by silence.

I recall walking directly up to your bedroom and opening the drawer of your nightstand to find your phone book. I remember how each of us divided the book into sections, so we would all have a part in telling your friends and family about your death. Together we called every name in your book. One by one we found ourselves breaking the news, breaking hearts, and breaking silences, some that may have gone on for years.

I remember how anger was the most prominent emotion confronting me at the time. I found myself wrestling with my anger towards God for taking you so hastily. I remembered my rage at the doctors for not letting me stand by your bedside while they performed compressions on your heart. I was angry at the friends and relatives who sat wordlessly on the other end of the telephone line not knowing what to say. I know they were in shock, just as I was. I know it was late and my call came from out of the darkness after a quiet and otherwise ordinary night. But ire was still the prominent emotion I felt in my heart.

One call in particular upset me the most. It was your friend Beverly. She had already heard the news from another friend, and while she was kind, she also sounded a bit stern:

"I'm sorry for your loss," she said. But then she quickly added, "You know I can't come to the funeral or to the *shiva*. I told your sister already that I have tickets to go to Aruba and it is the only week I can go. I'll be gone all week."

"You're not going to my mother's funeral?" I asked.

"I've had these plans a long time and I already postponed them once before," she explained. "Remember, Norman, that when your father died years ago, my husband and I had plans to go to Las Vegas, but we postponed them to go to *his* funeral."

I sat quietly and thought of what she must have been feeling. I told myself that she was sad, and that she probably couldn't face the reality of your death. And then I thought about what you would say.

"Beverly is struggling with cancer, Norman. She's got her own *tzurris*, her own worries. Leave her be. It's too hard for her to be there at my funeral."

"Yes, Mom, you are right. I realize you are right. But it's still so hard for me to forgive," I responded.

"Leave her be," you said. "Just leave it be."

And I did, Mom. I wished your friend a nice trip. I acknowledged her words of sympathy toward me and our family, and I told her that I would get in touch with her at some point in the not too distant future. And I thought about how you always tried to teach me to rise above "other peoples' nonsense."

I open my eyes from this flashback and I realize that I am standing at the top of the high school track. Angry and confused, I descend the steps of the old school yard and onto the track, and I commit to run as far and as fast as I can.

As I begin my run, I think of the friends that are probably arriving at your house at this very minute, compassionate and eager to pay their respects to our family. And with anger in my heart, I run faster, yelling voicelessly at all of them, every well-meaning comforter who I believe has little understanding of what any of us is really going through. The sun is high in the early September sky and I imagine you telling me not to rush to your house.

"Take your time, Norman. You've got a long week ahead of you. Take care of yourself. You'll get there when you can."

I feel the sun on my face and I attempt to use this third day of *shiva* as an exercise in self-care and personal discovery. I run with determination, and I record every emotion in my heart and every thought in my mind. Wind and tears blend into one, and I plead and argue with you and God and all of fate. Lap after lap my ire rises, and I ask myself if there is really any order in the universe. I hunt for your signs as I wrestle with my anger. I attempt to make peace with God, and with you, with the doctors and with your friends and relatives. After miles and miles of reckoning, I stop, resting wearily at the edge of the track.

It is hours later when I arrive at your house, and I am tired. Judi, Robert and Scott are all engrossed in conversations with visitors. I see our neighbors and I see *The Shiva Sisters* and I recognize the faces of people I have not seen in years. And then I see your beautiful glass dining room table covered with a plastic blue tablecloth.

"What's with the blue tablecloth?" I ask one of the *Sisters*.

"I thought it would be easier to clean up at the end of the day," she says to me.

"But my mother used white linen and lace," I tell her.

"Couldn't find any lace," she concedes.

"So we'll find it," I say. "Did you look in her linen closet, the drawers upstairs, the laundry room?"

"What's the difference?" she says. "It's easier with plastic."

"My mother would be devastated to have all of her friends come through this house with this plastic blue tablecloth in the center of it all."

"But I think it's nice," she says.

"Fine!" I say. "Then at your *shiva* I'll make sure to use blue plastic. But this is my mother's *shiva*, and my mother used linen."

And suddenly I look around and see in everyone's face that "I did it" again. I lost my cool and started yelling at my siblings, at their friends, and even at strangers. The sad road that brought us all to this place has culminated in my anger and disrespect, and I cannot seem to get through it.

Your friend Larry approaches me. With his hand on my shoulder, he pulls me close. "Listen," he says. "Your parents are dead and your sister and brothers are all you have now. No fights," he urges. "And when you sit down at the table to decide who gets what: the furniture, the jewelry, the pictures, I want you to remember that your mother and father are sitting with you, to your right and your left. No fights, you understand?"

"Yes, Larry," I say. "I understand." And I retreat to my backyard hammock and try to figure out how we are all going to see this week through to its ritually determined end. I close my eyes and flash back to just two months ago when you and I sat together and discussed how you wanted your things to be shared evenly among all of us.

"I have revised the will that your father and I had from years ago. It's the same as before, only I changed a few small details," you said. "And I want to make sure that it all makes sense. So read it."

"You want me to read your will, Mom?" I ask. "There's no need to go over this now," I begged.

"You never know," you advised. "Look it over and tell me if the lawyers made any sense with this thing."

And then you went on proudly telling me all that you had done to make the execution of your will easier for us.

"I had the house painted," you said. "It looks so beautiful and clean inside. And I put a new roof on and I had the bathroom ceiling fixed. Nothing fancy. Just plasterboard and white paint. But everything is clean and fresh inside. You should have no problem selling it. And the jewelry … I want all three girls to split it up among themselves: Judi, Robert's wife and your wife. You all divide it evenly. There's enough for everyone."

"Where are you going so fast?" I ask. "You'll probably outlive us all."

"You never know," was your answer. "You never know."

I open my eyes, get up from the hammock and climb the backyard stairs. As I enter your house through the kitchen, I see that more food has arrived. Today there are kosher tacos and burritos, chips and salsa, lemon chicken on wooden skewers, chopped liver and cucumber salad, two platters of deli meats, potato salad and coleslaw, designer cupcakes and fancy chocolates, trays upon trays of bakery cookies, and a bottle of wine. Scores of people seem to be surrounding your kitchen table deciding what they'll have for dinner later tonight. And all I think to myself is, "No popcorn. No one brought popcorn."

I walk into the living room and resume my place on my *shiva* box and wait for someone to comfort me, or admonish me because of my outburst. Shoshanna, your neighbor, gently approaches with freshly made humus from her quiet kitchen next door. She sees in my eyes that I am worn and confused, and she leans into me and whispers in Hebrew into my ear.

"*Tochal, motek.* Eat up, sweetheart. You look tired."

And with this kind gesture, I begin to cry. I realize that the smallest acts of kindness move me in ways both brilliant and unexpected. And in the midst of my tears I discover how my anger, how everyone's anger, is merely a blanket of wasted energy that covers and overwhelms more vulnerable feelings of fear, loss and insecurity. I forgive myself for my rage and I try to understand what it is that anger is trying to teach me. Is this a lesson in tolerance? I wonder. Is this about the need for patience, or compassion for others around me? Once again the answers elude me and I resolve to stop asking questions.

Shoshanna and Henry are lovely people, Mom. I wonder if you knew how kind and generous they are. Living next door to you for thirty years, I hardly heard you and Dad speak of them. But they are here, today and every day, like guardians watching over us and making certain that we are well and rested and prepared for the days ahead. They are hurting too, this I see. Your death was a shock to them as well. I remember how Shoshanna came running up your stairs the day before your funeral.

"What happened?" she asked us incredulously. "I just heard your message on my machine. We were away all weekend. What happened?" she pleaded.

"Mom died," we answered. "Suddenly and without warning. It started right there on the floor by the upstairs landing," I said. And with a turn of my head my eyes directed her to the top of the steps.

"But she was well," she added. "I saw her on Thursday, before I left. I asked her if she needed anything. But she said she needed nothing. Stubborn your mother was. Maybe I pushed too much. Who knows, maybe she felt I was in the way too often."

And she stood there, incredulous to the news.

I tell myself that I will stay in touch with Shoshanna. Somehow a connection to her seems like a connection to you. Maternal and loving, she holds within her memories and moments of you that I never got to see. I think of you pulling your little black Mercedes into the driveway and waving hello as she passed by on her way to do her errands. I imagine you talking to one another as you met by the edge of your respective driveways, piling bags of trash, one atop the other, on mornings when the garbage trucks came. I fantasize that she was awake and watching you as you entered your empty house on nights when you came home late from dinner with a friend, and I tell myself that you were never really alone after Dad died.

As I think of that black Mercedes, I am reminded of the last time you parked it in the garage. I was told that you had just come home from having your nails manicured and, leaving the driver's side door open, you entered into your house. You climbed the stairs, leaving your cane and your shoes on the bottom step. The paramedics told me that they found orange juice out on the table and half of a cookie by your side. Sugar, Mom? Was it sugar you craved? Were you suddenly feeling dizzy or lightheaded?

I was informed that you crawled your way up the second flight of stairs to your office – the office that used to be my bedroom. I was told that you called Judi from the desk phone in that room.

"Come quickly," you urged her. "Something is wrong. I don't feel well."

I was told that, only minutes later, Judi arrived to find you lying on the bedroom floor. The telephone was dangling off of its cradle, and you were barely conscious.

I tell myself that you felt no pain. I tell myself that you must have been tired, or a bit dizzy, and that you simply needed to lie down for a while. I lie to myself every time I think of that sad hour, and sometimes I believe my lie. Sometimes I believe that you felt nothing, that you were just weak and tired. I comfort myself by saying that by the time the paramedics arrived you were unconscious, unaware of them compressing on your heart. I tell myself that you didn't feel them pounding, sweating as they tried to revive you.

I remember hearing the sound of the sirens bluntly whirring from the inside of the ambulance chamber. I heard it all through the cell phone that connected Judi to me, she by your side, me hiding in my laundry room, helpless to the words of the paramedics as they said, "We lost her. I think we lost her."

I remember running into the emergency room twenty or so minutes later. I recount over and over in my mind how I didn't know if I would find you breathing and alive, or weightless in death. I recall the feeling of relief as they brought me to the foot of your bed and told me that you were breathing on your own, but still "very critical." I saw your toes turn faintly blue in color. "Necrosis is setting in," I told myself. "Your feet have no oxygen now. Your heart must be giving way." I remember seeing them slap your forearm over and over again, and I recall the sounds from the monitors as they beeped and whirred and measured your breath.

"Breathe, Mom. Breathe," I said.

But I saw that time was running out. I knew that God, in His wisdom, had a different plan. Life, your life, stellar and blessed, gilded and glorious, had reached its inglorious end. "So unexpected, so sudden and sad," I thought. And I stood there peeking through the curtain the doctors had pulled to give you privacy, brokenhearted and weary from a battle I never wanted to fight.

Did you feel them pressing on your heart? Did you hear me voice-lessly screaming as I stood on the dirty hospital floor, begging you to breathe?

But there on your shoulders I saw wings. I sensed the thirst of another love. Dad was there and he said, "Come, Selma. Come to me." And who was I to stop such a glorious display of heavenly love? Who was I to stop you at the gates of your finest hour? How dare I say, "Don't go"? He wanted you. You've done your job. It was your time to go.

I remember seeing the doctors pull away the bag that helped you breathe. I watched as they pulled away the hands that compressed and forced life back into you. And I saw that you were finally free.

★

I open my eyes and I realize that I am back in your house of *shiva*. The crowd is quieting down and someone is setting your table for dinner. The table is covered with a lace tablecloth. "Nice," I say to myself. "Someone understands."

I rise from my *shiva* box and walk into your dining room. Food is moving from room to table and from table to mouth. People I hardly know are eating food that was meant for your children. I walk around in confusion and despair, trying to remember all of the dinners we had here at your table. When you were here, we ate quietly and with honor and respect to the food you worked so hard to prepare. But now, here at your table, I see strangers laughing and drinking and swallowing, and ire grows deep within me. I tell myself to "be good," as you would have wanted. But I find myself feverishly, involuntarily, cleaning up around all these foreign faces.

"We have to move all of the meats into the kitchen," I command. "People will be flooding the house any minute now and my mother would not be happy with all of these cold cuts sitting out."

No one hears me, or so I think. So I continue to remove the half-eaten pieces of lemon chicken that lay strewn about your table. I tell myself to put up the coffee and to bring out the desserts. That's what you would have done.

But as I clean, someone approaches me and demands that I stop.

"Enough!" he yells. "Stop taking food away from us. Let people eat. We'll clean it all later."

Stunned, I stand there as if in someone else's house, not the house in which I grew as a child. Empty of memory, I stand inside my anger and confusion and I realize that this is the first day of many in which I will fight with my family and friends. And I accept that anger, and all of its attendant, negative outcomes, is an important part of *shiva*, too. Unwelcome and unkempt, ire has found us, and we are here to learn what we can from its presence.

Evening descends and I retreat to my box. I sit in silence and I pray for you to comfort me. I see people coming and going before my eyes. Teams of people: some are laughing, some are gossiping, and some are consoling the ones who are sad. The room spins with the noise of laughter and sorrow, love and compassion, but anger is all I feel. I tell myself that I am parentless now. I swear I heard some well-meaning comforter say that to me only moments ago. I am dizzy with opinions and objections and unanswered questions. And I sit quietly, pressed in my anger and silenced by the magnitude of it all.

I barely have the strength to rise for another evening prayer service. "New rabbi tonight," I say to myself. Same old prayers, but a new face to guide us through the age-old customs. I stand, I bend in requisite supplication, and I say the words aloud with my family. But I am not really here tonight.

★

I open my eyes and realize that the evening services have come to a close. People are hurriedly taking their leave, saying their goodbyes, offering their prayers of comfort, and promising to keep in touch. I hug those who came to comfort me, I say goodbye to my siblings, and I, too, make my way to your door. Time for me to head home as well, I tell myself. Tomorrow is another day. I wonder what lessons you will have for me to learn as the sun rises.

I am grateful for the events of this day, the good and the bad. I resolve to befriend my ire as I would any other emotion that stirs within. Like a welcomed souvenir from a life well lived, I commit to wrestle with anger in the hope of transforming it into something positive and self-expanding. I realize that I have much to learn and I thank you, for even in death you continue to teach.

## *Postscript*

WHAT CAN BE said about the meaning of anger, and what role does anger play in our eventual recovery from grief? We know that, as humans, we are capable of experiencing a full range of feelings, and that each of our emotions is inexorably connected to its opposite. We know that an honest life insists upon the wholeness, as well as the integrity of our emotions, thus an attachment to one feeling at the expense of others can have damaging effects on our growth. We understand that sorrow, pain and intolerance have a place in our lives, and we expect that, at times, they will be rivaled with joy, humility and compassion. Anger, too, has its place in our emotional world, and once explored and understood, it may indeed meet its own negation.

Like all other emotions, anger is a unique subjective experience. It is a reaction to our perception of specific events and the conclusions we draw from them. Regardless of whether our view is accurate or distorted, we know that anger's impact on our inner world will be profound. For most of us, it will generate changes in physical sensations, including increased heart rate and muscle tension, shallow breathing and disruptions in sleep and appetite. For others, anger will promote feelings of guilt, shame, self-loathing and even depression. Neurophysiology research suggests that anger can create cognitive changes, such as errors in reasoning or judgment, poor concentration, and strong feelings of helplessness. Anger also engenders changes in our social world, prompting withdrawal, bigotry or racism.

However, anger can have a profound impact on our spiritual development as well. Many angry grievers among us are likely to experience a reduction of faith in oneself, in religion, in God, or in a general sense of meaning and purpose in life. Anger forces us to confront the contradictions inherent in our existence – that we are strong and weak at the same time. Bereft and angry, we are challenged to forfeit, at least for a while, our belief in a neatly arranged world where order and justice prevail. It seems as if our prayers have been ignored, and we feel no reason to believe anymore. "What kind of God lets this happen?" we ask. The answer is unclear, and in the absence of meaning or pattern, anger leaves us spiritually dissatisfied and helpless. In the words of one mourner:

> We are taught that, if you live right and honor God, then you will have all of the blessings and miracles that are promised to those who believe and who keep the faith. But then you suffer an unexpected and untimely death; or a devastating medical diagnosis and the pain of its effects, and you lose hope for the future you once dreamed of, and are instead, left with anger and depression.

The relationship between anger and spiritual well-being has been expounded upon in the Talmud. Shimon ben Lakish, regarded as one of the second century's most prominent codifiers of Jewish oral tradition, stated that if a sage were to get angry, his wisdom would leave him, and if a prophet were to get angry, his prophecy would leave him. He expounded that Moses, "angry at the generals and captains" (Numbers 31:14), forgot the rule that God commanded him, thus requiring Eleazar the priest to state the law to the soldiers. In addition, when "Eliav (David's older brother) became angry with David" (1 Samuel 17:28), Eliav was stripped of his rank or "stature" as God "rejected him" (ibid., 7).

This does not mean that anger in itself is a base and unacceptable emotion. Quite the contrary, anger may become the motivating force for noble and valuable action, and eventual enlightened thought. Indeed, the Bible is abound with examples of stern, even ruthless action taken against injustice, as in the story of the ten plagues in Egypt and the flood that caused Noah to build his ark. Whether understood as direct teaching, or as metaphor for the totality of the human emotional experience, the Bible is suggesting to us that ire, when left detached and unexamined, is damaging to the soul, whereas active opposition, initiated through righteous anger, is a core component of a sincere and honest emotional life. Indeed, in his famous third chapter, *Kohelet* (3:2–8) gave poetic expression to the welcome continuum of our changing emotions:

> To everything there is a season, and a time to every purpose under the heaven . . . a time to love, and a time to hate; a time of war . . . and a time of peace.

Thus the Torah teaches us that the whole range of the emotional spectrum is present in each one of our affective experiences. Anger, like all other emotions, is a multi-level state of arousal whose own negation rests at the opposite end of the emotional continuum. Left unexamined and confined within the self, anger can cause us to withdraw and to remain isolated, never allowing our lives to become suffused with moral significance or healing potential. Indeed, like any emotion in isolation of its opposite, unexamined anger will preempt our human ability to experience the full cycle of affective life. When we leave our anger unexplored, we create self-loathing, which psychologists have long considered a precursor to depression. But when we focus on the emotions that lay beneath our anger, we begin to develop ways to help others and feel good about ourselves. As the Rav asserts, we must indeed know how to love and to hate, to understand the art of reaching out to others in need, and the craft of resisting and opposing injustice and wrongdoing.

Understood in this way, anger, along with all other disjunctive emotions, carries within it the seeds of its own repair. Indeed, psychologists have long studied the nature of guilt and its charge as a gateway to a greater and richer life, and the experience of remorse has been the catalyst of emotional and spiritual renewal for many religious groups. What, then, is the antithesis of anger, and what is required of us in order to achieve its nobler end?

The answer may lie in the Judaic tenet that critical awareness of our emotions ultimately endows them with meaningfulness. In our desire to be like God, to "walk in His ways" (Deuteronomy 28:9), we must fashion our deeds after Divine design. We are not a people who keep our feelings and actions confined to ourselves, but rather, we are asked to direct our emotional life toward the other, or the "Thou," as Jewish philosopher Martin Buber asserts. A self-centered emotional life begs enlightenment. Introverted and confined emotions must mingle with the outside, or we will lose our ability to see others as who they truly are. And, as the Talmud says, if you want to be seen, you must first see; if you want to be known, you must know others. But, in order to know others and find meaning in the world, we must first know ourselves.

Self-examination, however, especially as it pertains to anger, can be a frightening experience. As Martin Buber asserts, the deed involves sacrifice and risk (*I and Thou*, p. 60). The sacrifice: that which we hold as "true" about ourselves, even on an unconscious level, must be confronted and possibly surrendered. And when we confront the truth behind anger, we discover that we are actually vulnerable, frightened and helpless. The risk: the feelings we explore must be experienced with our whole being. We will not succeed if we seek respite in denial or lies. Thus, when we explore our anger, we risk feeling uncomfortable, uncertain and alone. We are forced to face the contradictions in our life: We want to see ourselves as strong, but we fear we are weak. We want to effect change in our world, but we feel powerless to our own fate. We have been betrayed, promises were broken, and our faith was challenged. As one mourner described:

> I thought I had it all: a great home, a high paying job and a happy family. Every night before I went to sleep, I checked on my kids and felt safe because they were all well, and asleep in their beds. And then my mother died, and now I am left feeling weak and unsure. I can't hold on to the future anymore because I feel like the future doesn't belong to any of us.

Afraid and despairing, many of us thus shut down from our emotions. We run from our feelings, seal off thoughts and desires that are too hard or too frightening to bear. Like Jacob running from his brother and nemesis Esau, some of us hide from our inner emotions for years. But, as the Torah teaches, even Jacob, alone and afraid of the impending confrontation with his enemy, was required to "wrestle until the breaking of the day" (Genesis 32:25).

Some interpret the famous story of Jacob wrestling with the angel as a metaphor for the internal struggle in each of us. The night is long and our work is hard, and, like the "strained hollow" of Jacob's thigh, none of us are left unscathed. And yet we continue to wrestle. Like Jacob, we commit our earthly selves to a struggle with our heavenly selves. We submit our more human side – our mortal feelings of fear and rivalry, jealousy and rage – to a struggle with our spiritual side, which contains the traits of love and kindness, compassion and concern for others. Which side of us will prevail? Which will be redeemed through our dark night?

The answer can be found in the story of Jacob, for the Torah tells us that, as the dawn broke, Jacob said to the angel:

> I will not let you go unless you bless me ... and [the angel] blessed him there. (ibid., 33:30)

We are also told that Jacob called this place of struggle "*Peniel*," which translates as "The Face of God." We learn from this portion that, after confronting our inner, mortal fears, and wrestling with our outer, more numinous side, we may finally become capable of seeing the "other," the "Thou" in front of and all around us. Our struggle to understand ourselves, and to understand others, forces us to succumb to love, for indeed, Jacob bowed seven times before his estranged brother and enemy, and the two ultimately embraced (ibid., 33:4). Fraught with tension and unrest, this embrace is complicated for the Torah and its commentators, and it suggests that the negation of anger through acts of loving-kindness is a human task whose ultimate goal is not easily, if ever, achieved.

In wrestling with our anger then, we ultimately learn that the earthly wish to be seen is only granted once we achieve the heavenly goal of seeing *first*. Only once we direct our eyes inward, and retreat into the abstruse darkness of the self, will we be able to see our anger as a cover for other disjunctive, more unwelcome feelings. And only once we direct our eyes outward toward the world and its people, with all of their fears and vulnerabilities, their sorrows and insecurities, will we perhaps be able to transcend our anger, embrace our foe, and see the face of God (*Peniel*).

One mourner, who lost her mother suddenly, describes this transcendence in the following way:

> I see my anger as loving, pure and honest. It is the crescendo of the story of my grief. I am open and vulnerable and fresh and true to my mother's love. It is the most committed love there is, present in heart and ancient in understanding, like words that float off of a page hovering and connecting me to two worlds. I look for that love in the eyes of others: her friends, my friends, people who shared my mother and who see me as I truly am. And when I am in the presence of such a person, I realize that my other sees me still.

Esther Chasin, author of *Mitzvoth as Spiritual Practices*, refers to this process as "*hesed*," which is defined as a "loving nature," and the inner force that overrides our temptation to judge others harshly. Chasin warns us to consider the judging of others, as well as of ourselves, as an ineffective response to introspection. Judgment, she says, preempts our true nature to be considerate and compassionate. It thwarts our ability to, in the words of the great scholar Hillel, treat others as we would want to be treated ourselves. Through anger we lose the ability to deal patiently and with understanding, and we judge others by their wrongdoings or by their misguided acts alone. We must thus use the indomitable spirit of self-discipline (*gevurah*) to hear the voice of loving-kindness, and courageously ignore the voice of the ego.

The dialectic of anger is thus: Anger limits us from seeing – whether it is the sight of Divine influence, or the influence of others around us. It's opposite, *hesed*, or true loving-kindness, allows us to see ourselves and the "other." Anger causes us to protect ourselves, and to run for emotional cover. *Hesed* compels us to use Divine influence to perfect ourselves, and to address our fellow man and teach him what our suffering is teaching us. Anger causes emotional withdrawal and spiritual contracting, whereas *hesed* promotes, as the Jewish Mystics say, existential expansion.

Through our dark night of struggle, we thus discover that we are *in need* as much as we are *enraged*. We reach inward and wrestle with our sorrow and pain, and we attempt to invoke its antithesis. We turn outward through acts of *hesed* and loving-kindness and explore ways to feel good about others. We begin to examine our self worth, and we discover what makes us unique and special. We allow healthy pride to develop and, with this pride, we are more able to help our fellow man, while allowing our fellow man to help us.

The Rav describes this great act of our loving-kindness as containing two features. First, we must bear the "communal yoke" and participate in the trouble and grief of the community. Second, we must empathize with another sufferer by identifying with his pain; we must feel a sense of responsibility for his fate. Thus, when we are in the presence of someone like Jacob, who wrestled with Laban, and Esau and the angel at the river (ibid., 32:23–32), we offer him compassion and advice. We make a plea on his behalf, and pray for the fulfillment of his needs so that he may redeem himself from his own isolation and anger. And as we do this, we find ourselves rejoining the community, transforming our anger into care and concern for others who are hurt like us. We relate to the man of sorrow with prayer and loving-kindness, and he relates to us likewise, as we both pass through the multitude of life's tribulations.

The Rav states that prayer is the "linking of one soul to another and the fusing of tempestuous hearts." In prayer, we bring the "I" closer to the "Thou." Prayer connects us as individuals with the community. It elevates us from personal self-concern and self-confinement to a union with the suffering world as a whole. Like Job, who, after all of his travails, finally understood the true nature of prayer – that its plural voice sweeps man from private pain to a public abode – so too our struggles with anger can release us from the prisons in which we find ourselves. Indeed it is written:

And the Lord changed the fortune of Job, when he prayed for
his friends; and the Lord gave Job twice as much as he had
before. (Job 42:10)

Thus, anger, with its attendant struggle and sorrow, can ultimately
help to redeem us. For in raising us to a level of *hesed*, loving-kindness,
and true concern for others, we begin to heal what is broken inside
ourselves.

# *Valor*

Mом,

It is Thursday, the fourth day of your *shiva,* and I have decided to go to morning services in my own synagogue, as well as to have *shiva* in my own house today. I have many friends in the neighborhood and, just as you would expect of me, I want to make it easier for some of them to visit. But I have decided to "sit" here for another reason: I want the boys to see how *shiva* is done in the house in which they are growing up. I want all three of them, even Davey, to have a memory of the time their father honored you, here, after your death.

Every day they come to your house and run around in your basement, they swivel on your chairs and bounce on your furniture, and they eat the food that continues to arrive, almost hourly, to your kitchen. But soon we will have to sell your house. Soon enough we will be packing fifty years of memory into boxes, some of which will include this long week of *shiva.* My siblings and I have not yet spoken about that process. We walk around with heavy hearts, all of us unwilling and afraid to open a dialogue about selling.

It's a beautiful house: soothing and peaceful. I am certain that each of us has our own personal memories rooted deep within its walls. I know for myself that my memories of the past mingle with the present day every time I visit. I see Davey playing in the corner of the basement that used to be my favorite space for hide and seek. I watch as Josh and Jacob try in vain to blow into Dad's old tuba, and I think of how Scott and I used to do the very same thing when we were children. I look at everything you have saved from our childhoods and I realize that I want to do the same thing for my kids in my home. So, today, it is here in my house where I wish to honor you.

Morning prayers are different in the synagogue in my town. I see my own friends and colleagues, not the men and women with whom you and Dad prayed when we were young. I realize today that, once your *shiva* is over, I will probably never return to your synagogue again. And I see now how you and Dad were the force that drew us all together for prayer and family tradition.

When I return from saying the morning prayers, I find that Beth has cleaned the house beautifully. An urn full of coffee is already percolating on the center island in the kitchen, Styrofoam cups stacked neatly in a row, sugar and milk exactly where you would have placed them. I see that two large baskets of bagels and cream cheese have already been delivered from the hospital where I work, and a low stool has been placed in the back of the living room, right in front of a picture of you and Dad in a silver frame.

I am overcome by all that Beth is doing in her attempt to make this process as bearable as possible. I am grateful and guilty at the same time, because I know she hurts too. You were a good mother to her, a woman of valor, and she blossomed from your love. She tells me often how you were the only person who remembered to call her after each of our children's doctor visits, every first haircut, first tooth and first day of school. She reminds me of how you prepared for them all of the foods we were loathe to make, and of how you never missed a chance to buy them all matching winter coats, mittens and hats, and pajamas.

Your death has permeated so many boundaries. Your children and grandchildren, your friends and neighbors, the members of the synagogue, store owners from the places you shopped. Even the woman who did your nails was touched by your passing. I remember how I saw her standing uncomfortably in the corner of the chapel on the day of your funeral. I recall how she stood there, talking to no one, watching as all of your friends gathered together to console one another. I remember how, when the crowds finally thinned, she approached me.

"I am so sorry for your loss," she said to me. "I am your mother's manicurist. I was with her only two hours before she died." And I saw in her eyes how sorry she was, how sad she was to have to be the person to carry such a burden.

"What was my mother like?" I asked her. "Was she complaining of pain?"

"She was tired," she answered. "She was so tired. And she was sad."

"Sad?" I asked.

"Yes. Sad," she conceded. And then, carefully, she added, "Your mother was worried that the procedure she had last week at the hospital did nothing to help her. She said that she was feeling pain in her back, and she worried because she felt as if she still couldn't do all of the things she wanted to do. She knew something was wrong, I think. I told her to think of her children. She loved you all."

Is it true that you were sad, that you knew something was wrong? Standing there in front of this woman, I became confused. I told myself that she was wrong, that she was overcome by the grief that surrounded her, and all of us, on the day of your funeral. I told myself that her limited knowledge of the English language made her misunderstand your words, that she was mistaken. But every so often I wonder and worry that she was correct.

I am in need of distraction from all of these memories, so I go for a run. The track is empty on this early September morning; everyone seems to be away for the Labor Day weekend. I start my run, picking up the pace fast and feverishly. Music in my ears, I think about the days that have passed, and about the days still ahead. This seven-day exercise in grief and honor has overwhelmed me and filled me with contrasting thoughts and emotions. I imagine how it will be once *shiva* is over and all of the promises that friends have made are finally revealed. I think of your devoted neighbors, and wonder if they'll visit us in our respective homes. I wonder if *The Shiva Sisters* will stay in touch, and I think about the upcoming holidays without you.

Faster and faster I run, fighting off feelings of emptiness and dread, fears of abandonment, as well as anger and disbelief. I find myself beginning to breathe heavily. As tears fall on my face and the sun rises, I begin to plead.

"Why?" I yell. "Why?"

I ask the question over and over and I run even faster around the high school track. I want to hear you offer me an answer. "Any answer, Mom. Anything will do," I tell myself. But even in my rage and grief I know there is no answer. "What were you thinking, Mom? You left us without a goodbye. Why?"

I think back on childhood mornings when I heard you say goodbye as I ran after the school bus, or afternoons I left the house for play rehearsal, or nights when I would go out with friends. I think of the goodbye you would say every time I packed my sleeping boys in the car after Sunday night dinners at your house.

"Drive safe," you'd say.

"Safe*ly*," I'd say silently to myself. And then I'd turn and watch you close the door to your house, your smile turning to tears, wishing we lived closer or visited more often.

I begin to run slowly and my breathing becomes heavy. My hands are tingling, and my lower arms are beginning to feel numb. Nearly out of breath, I run home. I am met at the door by all three of my sons and they see me fall into Beth's arms as I cry. Stilled by feelings of confusion and fear, they all three stand at attention.

"Let them see me cry," I tell myself. "Let them learn firsthand about how a man grieves. Let them see it all," I say to myself.

Suddenly, little Davey approaches me and, with an outstretched hand, he says, "Don't cry, Daddy." I hug him and thank him for his gesture of kindness. And I say to all three of them, "This is grief, boys. I miss Grandma and this is how I grieve. This is what grief looks like, and sounds like."

Shyly, Jacob approaches my side and, with a sad look on his face, says, "I miss her too, Daddy."

"Stop faking," screams Josh. "Those aren't real tears and you know it."

"Josh, sometimes people cry with tears. And sometimes they cry with laughter, or anger," I explain. "Let Jacob cry in any way he wishes."

"What is heaven like, Daddy?" Jacob asks.

Curious to know his thoughts on where his grandmother has gone, I return the question back to him:

"I think heaven is like living inside of a video game," he replies. "It's like this beautiful place that has everything you want in it: games, and fishing poles, and skis."

"And where is Grandma?" I ask.

"Grandma is sitting with God, who is on a rocking chair. And God is playing a banjo, and Grandpa is dancing next to her," he answers.

"I think heaven is like life #2," Josh chimes in. "Not day #2 or year #2, but life #2. And when we die we will go to be with Grandma in our life #2." He adds, "She'll be there waiting for you, Daddy. Don't worry."

At age nine, Josh is able to understand the permanence and universality of death. I see how his mind is struggling to make sense of both the science and the spirituality behind this whole ordeal. And as we sit there in the foyer of our house, I realize that my children, each of them in their own unique and young ways, are learning how grief changes us all. I am grateful for this family that understands and embraces me in my sadness. I am grateful for the days you showed me with your tears that it was healthy to cry. And I am grateful to be able to pass your lessons along to my children.

"I'll be ok boys," I assure them. "I will be just fine. I will cry sometimes, and then I will dry my eyes and laugh. This is how I will grow, how we will all grow through this sad time."

And with that, Jacob starts to tell me a story about how his favorite cartoon character cried once. Deeper and deeper he delves into the story, and Josh corrects him at every possible misremembered moment. And they begin to laugh as they reenact the silly things they remember seeing in that cartoon. And even though I don't find the humor in much of their story, I laugh anyway. I laugh loudly and I thank them all for helping me to smile again. I kneel down onto my knees and thank each of them one by one, and I imagine you standing there behind me, smiling along with all of us.

I walk over to my *shiva* stool at the back of the living room, close my eyes and let my thoughts travel. I think about my grieving patients, and I suddenly realize how much I have in common with many of them. I am struck by the recognition of how physical this grief is. It feels as if I am on the edge of something awful at every moment. Food seems unappealing, breathing is hard, and quiet moments are often filled with the physical sensations of dread and emptiness. Spiritually I am shaken as well. The world God created seems suddenly diminished in stature and size. I tell myself that the pain I feel represents a flaw in creation or some sort of cosmic injustice. And I sit here amidst these thoughts and feelings, and wait. I find myself waiting as if something is on its way, and I pray that it is comfort, not danger, that approaches next. I am trying to make peace with what is broken. I tell myself that, somehow, it will be repaired; somehow we will all be saved. And I remember a story a grieving patient once told me:

> When I was fifteen, my father and I were on a vacation and, passing by a dock with boats, I asked him if we could go sailing. We rented a little sailboat and took it out into the ocean. I set up the sail and we drifted out, tacking through the waves. I asked my father to help me, and he said, "You sail. I'll sit here and watch." And as we sailed, we began to take on more wind and more speed. Eventually we were so far out that I could see the breakers of the Atlantic. I turned to my father and I asked him for help. "We're in trouble," I told him. "I can't get us back to shore," I cried.
>
> "I have something to confess to you," my father said shyly. "I don't know how to sail."
>
> For a minute, I sat there frozen with fear. And then, without wasting any more time, I dropped the sail so we wouldn't take on any more wind. I turned the boat around and pointed it in the direction of home, and floated, waiting to be saved.
>
> "And what happened next?" I asked him.
>
> "Someone from the shoreline saw us floating and came out with a raft and saved us," he answered. Then, referring to his grief, he sadly added, "But now, as a grown man, I don't know how to save myself."
>
> "Yes, you do," I assured him.
>
> "How do you know that?" he asked me.
>
> "Because you were the one who put the sail down all those years ago," I answered. "Not your father. It was you who saved

yourself *and* your father. You did it then and you can do it now," I said.

"But how?" he asked.

"Put the sail down," I told him. "Stop searching further outside for comfort, distraction, or answers, and head for home. Let your family be the current that pulls you, and head for home."

And I realize that this is exactly what I need to do now. Like my patient, I am confused and afraid, uncertain as to where to go and how to save myself from the sadness that overwhelms me. And suddenly I realize that it is home to where I must turn. I see now that grief is asking me to have the courage to face the demands of needy children and a heartbroken wife, as well as the courage to ask for my own needs to be met. I am learning that I must find valor to bear the things that are the hardest: the lessons of being a husband and parent while still being in the midst of my own grief for you.

Breathing more calmly, and feeling more aware of the work that grief is asking of me, I open my eyes to see that friends have already started to gather in the kitchen. Exhausted from the run I never finished, and from all that has taken place since, I sit upon this stool and greet my friends. It is a quieter version of *shiva* at my house than it has been at your house, Mom. Everyone here has come to comfort me and Beth, and I am relieved to discover that I don't have to share my friends with any of my siblings. I don't have to make introductions or say hello to people I may not know. Instead, I can sit peacefully and tell stories about you as my friends listen attentively, and with care.

Calmly, I start to tell them about the lessons I am learning from you in the aftermath of your death. I tell them about my sadness and fatigue, and I talk of the moments of fear and dread. More and more friends and colleagues arrive, and as they gather, I see them quietly pick up in the middle of my story without asking questions. They may not even be interested in hearing all of it in its entirety, nor in hearing its resolution. And I realize that the telling of my story, with its sad and uncomfortable moments of rage and fear, is one of the healing powers in this trying week of *shiva*. I discover that whatever I say about you, and about me and my pain, has become my bounty to work with, to use toward growth and understanding.

I speak about you with a comfort I have rarely felt before, for few people here know you and they seem to want to learn more. They allow me to find your story's matching parts, both inside of me, as well as inside of themselves. I search out loud through the wreckage of the past week, hoping to find ancestral messages or buried memories, unexpected delights or long ago forgotten laughter. I feel comforted by the silent attention: a silence that is filled with patience and compassion. I recount many of the details of the night you died and I reveal my guilt for not getting to the hospital faster. I confess to my anger for wishing you had chosen a different, more "opportune" night to die. I concede to fears of attention and abandonment – overtures of companionship and support jarred by the realization of your sudden exit. I wrestle with feelings of jealousy as I imagine with whom among your children you were closest. And I allow my imagination to carry me through the moments still ahead.

I look up and find myself being introduced to a woman I have never seen before.

"Hello, Dr. Fried, I am your son's new kindergarten teacher." And I realize suddenly that today must have been Davey's first day of school. "Davey told me that his Grandmother died on Friday," she continues. "And I wanted to come by to say hello and to wish you my sincere condolences." And she hands me a quiche that she made from her kitchen.

"Thank you," I respond. "Has he said anything to you about his Grandmother?" I ask.

"Oh yes," she replies. And I listen as she tells me all about your littlest grandson's first day of school and what he understands of your death:

"Davey told me how his Grandma went to heaven to be with his Grandpa Dave. He told me that he never met his grandfather, that he was born right after his grandfather died, and that he was given his grandfather's name. He also said that you are sad and that you miss Grandma very much."

"Good job, Davey," I think to myself. "I taught you well and I see that you understand." And then I say out loud, "Thank you for coming, I am honored that you care." And I return to my chair, feeling relieved that Davey, like his two older brothers, is telling people in his world about you.

I look up and I see two of my patients suddenly standing before me: a married couple who come to me for help with parenting. They ask me about you, about the kind of mother you were, and about how I am managing through these days. I answer them, comfortably and with an intimacy I have never shared with them before. The wife tells me that she has only been an observer during *shiva*, that she was never comfortable speaking too much or staying in the house of mourning for too long. She describes how, not having lost a parent, she does not fully understand the mourning process. She admits that she was afraid to come at first, but that now she is grateful to sit and listen to my stories, as if "practicing, trying on, or playing follow-the-leader."

Quietly, she tells me what she is learning from my stories. She says that she believes it is good to be imperfect while we pass through this world because it makes us vulnerable and human. She tells me that she recognizes how brothers and sisters grow differently, and that even though they live separate and distinct lives, a mother loves them all. She says she pictures you, a woman she has never met, with arms outstretched around clear blue water as your "boats" float in to the harbor. She tells me that you are collecting us and protecting us and that we are always within your reach, and that this is the type of mother that she wants to be to her children. She tells me that she likes you because you are beautiful and flawed, and that she likes her own mother's flaws because they make her beautiful. She says all of this in response to the things I am telling her about you, Mom. And suddenly I realize that, like an intimate therapy session in my private office, *shiva* has rare moments where the one who comforts is healed just as much as the one who mourns.

I thank them for their kindness and I walk them to the front door. Beth comes to me and asks about the half hour that has just passed and, as I tell her, I see that she understands. I am struck by a changing view of my wife, for I realize that, like you, she is also a harbor. I recognize how she, too, is guiding our boats home. And so I thank you for reminding me about the sanctity of marriage and the healing power of family.

Evening comes and my house begins to stir with the sounds of friends, colleagues, and neighbors. Cakes and cookie trays are being delivered, coffee is being poured and platters of cold cuts are being opened and eaten. Beth is walking around thanking people for coming, and Josh and Jacob are running through the rooms, telling everyone they see about their first days of school. I am shocked by some of the people I see – faces of close friends and faces of acquaintances whose names I barely know. What a tribute, I tell myself. Everyone here wishes to pay their respects to a woman many have never even met. And I decide to remain seated on my *shiva* stool, afraid to leave this spot and accidentally walk past a visitor who came to comfort. I tell myself that if I sit right here all night, I can't be blamed for not approaching anyone.

And indeed, as I sit, a line forms before me. Friends seem to be waiting their turn to offer a kind word or a quick hug. There is a chair to my immediate right and my immediate left, and I discover that people are sitting for only a few moments in each, and then making way for the next two people in line. I am told that the line of comforters stretches through the kitchen, past the foyer, and out to the front of the house. And I am stunned and surprised by the multitude of friends and neighbors who are here, and by the speed with which this night is passing.

I find myself repeating my story over and over as new faces approach. With some, I elaborate, and with others I am concise. Some friends just wave to me from the back of the room knowing that they won't make it to the front of the line; others offer a simple touch as they walk past. My voice is weakening as I recount my memories and my feelings, and I find myself slumping lower in my chair as the hours pass.

The rabbi from my synagogue arrives and I realize that it is time for another evening prayer service. He has come with a *minyan* of ten congregants from the temple, but we are almost one hundred standing together, shoulder to shoulder. Prayer books are handed out, skullcaps are placed on heads, and everyone is asked to rise. I look around and watch as scores of people open the books they have been given and make their efforts to read along in English or in Hebrew. I think about the generations of people who have stood like this before, saying prayers and extolling God's virtues. I think about Dad and the nights he said the mourner's prayer for his mother and father as the four of us, his children, ran through his house, barely aware of the changes that were happening inside of him. I think about my siblings back at home, saying the very same prayers amongst their friends, your friends and our extended family. I am fascinated by the long embrace these words have formed from one house to the other, one generation to another. And I recognize the power in the rituals that we are forced to follow, sometimes blindly, but always with respect.

It is getting late, and people are slowly leaving as the house quiets down. I return to my stool and see my boss from the hospital where I work. I sit with him and we talk about the things people have said to me this week, about the difficult feelings and thoughts I have had, and about the lessons I am learning. We laugh and commiserate about the process, and I am surprised to discover that the man whom I always referred to as "Boss" feels more like a friend to me now. I thank him for helping me to laugh and for appreciating the challenges of *shiva*, and I escort him, and the last of the comforters, out of the house.

It is late now, but I am uninterested in sleep. I feel bad that I haven't been to your house at all today and I feel a need to go there. I help Beth clean up the mess that is left behind, kiss the boys goodnight, and decide to take the half hour drive to your house. I am guided by a feeling of warmth that I hope to receive by returning there. It's funny how I have missed only one day of *shiva* at your house this week, and already I feel separated from family and from you.

When I arrive, I see that it is quiet and still, the lights are off and the doors are locked. I let myself in and notice that everyone has gone to their homes to sleep. I climb the steps to your living room and sort through the remnants of the day that has passed without me. I see empty folding chairs neatly stacked in the corner, four *shiva* boxes leaning against the back wall of the room, platters of cookies and candy wrapped tightly in cellophane, stacks of paper cups and plates sitting off to one side of your glass dining room table, and piles of prayer books and condolence cards.

I enter your kitchen. There is so much food here: cold prepared meals, hot dishes now refrigerated, and a freezer filled with unopened food to be defrosted during the upcoming Jewish holidays. But none of it, hot or cold, reminds me of you. Nothing here, as well-intentioned as it all is in its presentation and offering, speaks of you and of our past. What I want to eat, what I really crave at this moment, is the taste of your homemade Rugelach cookies. I remember how you used to spend hours in the middle of the night rolling the dough and sprinkling it with cinnamon and sugar, chopped walnuts and raisins. I remember how you would sigh a heavy sigh of exhaustion the morning after, tired from standing through the night at that kitchen table, baking and assorting your special cookies to be served for dessert after holiday meals. It was an act of courage, Mom. Nurturing us taught me how to be heroic for my own family.

Impulsively, I clear the table of its boxes and paper plates, plastic cutlery and coffee urns. I rummage through the cabinets in search of your box of recipes. Not hard to find, I pull the card on which you inscribed the instructions for your famous Rugelach. Through faded words covered with dried flour and sugar, I read and decipher the materials I will need to bake those cookies and make myself feel closer to you. Half a pound of butter, 8 ounces of cream cheese, two cups of sifted flour, 1/3 cup of sugar, yellow raisins, chopped walnuts, chocolate cooking morsels, a pinch of salt, a dash of cinnamon, a rolling pin, a cutting board, a flour sifter, a measuring cup.

"Where is your measuring cup, Mom?" I say out loud.

I search every cabinet, every drawer, but it is nowhere.

"I didn't use a measuring cup, Norman," I hear you say to me. "You take a glass and estimate a cup's worth."

"I can't do that, Mom. I never made these cookies before."

But there I stand, mug in hand, trying desperately to figure what one cup of flour should look like.

"Don't make a mess in my kitchen," I hear you warn.

"I'll clean it all up, Mom. I promise."

I retrieve your old electric mixer from the back of the cabinet beneath your oven, dust it off, and place the worn out whisks in their respective ports. I pour all of the ingredients into the mixing bowl, turn the power button on, and start to make the dough.

"Make four balls," you instruct me. "And put them in the refrigerator."

An hour passes, maybe two, and I am covered with flour and memories of you. I know you are annoyed with the mess I am making, and I assume you disapprove of the way I roll the dough on the cutting board.

"You forgot to sprinkle flour on the rolling pin," you remind me. "Look at the mess . . . Oh Norman, what are you doing? There are boxes and boxes of cookies on the counter. Why do you need to start baking now?"

But I persist. It is the taste of your homemade food, not store bought and packaged, that I crave. And thus I remain focused. Cutting the pizza-shaped dough into twelfths, I sprinkle filling all around, and roll it "wide side first."

Suddenly I begin to see your splendid cookies take shape. Beautiful and delicate, each new Rugelach comes into view, swirls of cinnamon-spotted dough filled with sweetness and hard labor. And I smile, because I feel you here with me. And I know you are proud.

"Twenty minutes in the oven on three hundred and fifty degrees," I hear you say. "Watch until the edges start to turn golden brown."

"Yes, Mom. Thank you."

And I sit and wait. I wait for the minutes to pass, to take me far away from this time and place. I wait for relief from the sadness I feel inside, for you to tell me that everything will be alright. I wait for the world to slow down so I can once again rejoin the busy and the seemingly "un-afflicted." I wait for a friend to tell me that he understands, truly understands, all that I am going through. I wait for a sign that the path I am on is the right one. I wait for all of these things as I sit here in your warm kitchen, and I know that nothing will come to me in so short a time. I know that grief comes and goes in waves, with a pace all its own. I recognize that my emotions are not linear, that they more resemble a spiral staircase on which are recapitulated themes of anger, fear, shock and sadness. But still I wait.

The oven timer rings and I open the door. Pulling out the trays of freshly baked cookies, I notice that they are not exactly like the ones you made. They are sadly misshapen, lighter and smaller than those I remember from long ago. I taste the first one, dry and crunchy, and I smile, realizing that this will be the first of many things I do without your guidance.

And I see how I must acknowledge that all things, not just cookies, will take on a different shape now.

I place the cookies carefully on your favorite serving tray, each in its own paper wrapper. Covering the plate with cellophane, I add it to the pile of store-bought baked goods lining your kitchen counters. I clean up the mess I made, turn down the lights, and leave.

When I return home, I climb the quiet steps that lead to my boys' bedrooms. I enter their rooms one by one, and sit quietly by each sleeping child. I close my eyes and think of nights long ago when it was you who comforted me. I hear your footsteps as you gently enter my room and kiss me on my forehead. I smell you; I smell the scent of cold cream and perfume. I feel your hands, soft and cool, as they brush away the hair from my eyes, and you whisper in my ear. "Sleep tight, *Mama shana*. I'll see you in the morning light."

And now it is my turn to do what you have taught me, night after childhood night, so many years ago. I lean gently into each little face and kiss my boys, one by one, on their foreheads. And as I do, I feel you behind me. A woman of valor: you cover me like the shawl you wore on Sabbath nights, and you bless me like the candles you lit so long ago. I realize that I am blessed with the gift of generations, of memory and of the wisdom that can be found there. I think of all that is broken in the world, of all that God has left unfinished. I sit for a while and welcome in the silence, sails down, and headed for home, and I know I will be saved.

## *Postscript*

WHAT IS VALOR, and how does an understanding of it help us endure that which is void and empty in our hearts, as well as in the world? When we think of valor, we think of the concept of boldness and determination in the face of great danger, especially in battle. We think of heroic courage and bravery. The part of this definition that applies to most mourners is the last, for, as sentient beings, we know we must be brave if we are to survive our pain. "The day is long and the work is hard," the Sages tell us. And we are confronted daily, if not moment to moment, by the hardships of loss and despair. In the words of one mourner:

> For me, it is not enough to simply master the logistics of maneuvering through this new world. As difficult as that maneuvering is, it is actually the easier part of the journey. There are harder aspects of grief for me. Sometimes I fear I will have no courage to honor my loved one, that she will slip away from me because I will not be brave enough to hold on. I fear that the grief will suck everything out of me and I will become powerless to act. And then my mother will truly be gone.

Valor thus asks us to look inward to examine what it is we are most afraid of. It forces us to ask, "What is broken inside of us, as well as in the universe as a whole, that requires courage and determination, replenishment and repair?" We know that we live in an imperfect world where pain and sadness abound. Indeed, suffering and turmoil are as primordial as time for, as we read in the Book of Genesis, God built a world out of chaos and turmoil:

> The earth was unformed and void, and darkness was upon the face of the deep ... And the spirit of God hovered over the face of the waters and said "Let there be light." And there was light. (1:2)

Thus Judaism affirms the principle of creation out of nothingness. The void and the darkness, the chaos and the profane, were all fashioned before the orderly, the beautiful, and the majestic. Good and evil subsist through time, and both must dwell together within the cosmos.

However, we know the forces of iniquity, pain and chaos often exceed their bounds. They plunge back to the earth or emanate unbidden from within, transgressing the limits of goodness that God has set for man and nature. Like the raging sea, the waters of disorder lay waste to the beauty of creation, crashing down on the shores of health, family and safety. How then, do we invoke God's limit? How do we build and rebuild a harbor around the deep and the chaotic waters in an effort to preserve the principles of order and majesty? And how do we, as mourners, put our sails down in an effort to be saved?

The answer may be found through an appreciation of the work of creation as seen in the Book of Genesis. Indeed, Judaism believes that God gave us the Book of Genesis not for the sake of theoretical study alone, but also as a template upon which man can continue to perfect the act of creation. For in Genesis we learn that God created the world with an opportunity, if not a command, for man to participate and continue in His work. Indeed, we have already learned that Adam was given a mandate by God to "fill the earth and subdue it" (1:28), and that he was commanded to "cultivate it and keep it." (2:15). Later in Genesis we learn that, as soon as Abram attached himself to God, as soon as he understood and fashioned himself after God's words, and attempted to restore paradise on earth, God revealed Himself, changing his name to Abraham, and making a covenant with him:

> As for Me, behold, My covenant is with thee, and thou shalt
> be the father of a multitude of nations. (17:4)

Similarly, Lurianic Kabbalah, a sixteenth century mystical school that revolved around the teachings of Rabbi Isaac Luria, suggests that creation was a process by which God contracted the Divine Self in order to make room for goodness in the world. In the Lurianic creation story, God emanated His Divine Self into the world through ten vessels. Some of these vessels, too weak to hold the powers contained therein, shattered, resulting in a mixture of Divine Light with the shards of the vessels themselves. It is believed that, through this creation process, evil was introduced into the world. Thus, as Lurianic Kabbalah suggests, man must partner with God to redeem the world and to free the Divine Light from the broken shards of life. This attempt to free goodness from evil is known in Hebrew as *Tikkun Olam*," or repairing the world.

Thus Judaism teaches that, in order to replenish the deficiency in creation, man must possess the courage to become partners with God and fix what is broken. Like the waning moon, man sees the image and stature of creation as impaired and, with human hands, attempts to repair what is diminished and unjust so that he may become anointed with the crown of God's glory. In essence, the more man does to fix the world, the more he becomes like God. Through the act of creation, and the performance of *mitzvot* (religious commandments), as well as prayer and study, man carves an essential border between order and chaos, and separates existence from nothingness. Moreover, through partnering with God toward the perfection of the cosmos, man draws the Divine Presence, the *Shekhina*, downward into the material and suffering world, thus attaining the rank of holiness. As it says in Deuteronomy:

> For the Lord Thy God walkest in the midst of thy camp . . .
> therefore shall thy camp be holy, that He see no unseemly
> thing in thee, and turn away from thee. (23:15)

Perhaps the greatest partnership of all, and one which aids most in the replenishment of a holier, more "Divine" world, is the relationship between God and woman. For woman, who becomes mother (whether she is a biological or a psychological mother), is the progenitor of life, transmitter of covenantal law, and leader of the family. The Book of Proverbs dedicates its last section (31:10–31) to the "Woman of Valor" for whom her children rise up and call her blessed. As mother, she lives not only for herself, but for "the multitude" of others as well. She is concerned with the destiny of her children, and of the world in which they will grow and live. In partnership with God, woman is thus infused with a commitment to renewal, improvement and love for the world. Her relationship with her children endows her life with ethical meaning, and she becomes a teacher, a prophet, and a carrier of tradition and history. In the words of one patient:

> When my grandparents died, my parents gave me the holy
> books of my grandfather's mother. Some were so worn and
> without covers, they are stacked high away from hands, just

to rest. Upon receiving them, I gently searched these treasures wanting to feel my legacy. Finding one book marked, I immediately recognized that someone, likely my Great Grandmother (Bubbie), had mourned with this book in my hands. I felt so intimately a part of her, her weary hands, and her sadness. It was filled with the tears of my Bubbie's prayers. My Bubbie prayed for me. And at 36, I was now a mother myself, with hopes and dreams and vulnerabilities just like she had. And now I know that the past and the present are connected to share a moment.

With God as her partner, a mother teaches her children the biblical obligation of *kibbud*, which in English means "to honor one's parents." She knows that this commandment summons her children to act out a technique of good will directed from the innermost recesses of their psyche, and she understands that it will help them to establish relatedness and a spiritual closeness to God. The Rav says that behind every mother trails the *Shekhina*, and when one has the awareness of standing before God, one's holiness is consecrated. Thus, honoring thy mother is honoring God as well.

In families where two parents live together, a mother (and wife) stands side by side with the father of her children, creating an effective coalition. She honors the hopes and dreams of her spouse and she strives for the realization of a common goal between them. The two share a vision, though silently she recognizes that she is the determining influence in many situations. Indeed, as the Rav expounds from the Book of Genesis, a good mother is like Sarah, who is perhaps responsible for all of the accomplishments attributed to Abraham. She leads the leader and teaches the teacher. She interprets his dreams and guides him when he is lost. And yet, when her job is done, she retreats and remains shrouded in mystery. She is modest and humble, and her humility brings her the reward. Like Sarah who remained hidden from the three angels that stood before her tent, (Genesis 18:9), a mother receives God's mighty gift:

> And He said: "I will certainly return unto thee ... and, lo, Sarah thy wife shall have a son."(ibid., 18:10)

However, motherhood also involves pain and sorrow. As mother, woman must be strong and valorous, for she says "no" to the easy ways of life. She is involved in the act of creation, and is thus ready to surrender to the energy of the world. As it says in the Torah:

> Unto the woman He said: "I will greatly multiply thy pain and thy travail; in pain thou shalt bring forth children . . ." (ibid., 3:16)

But a mother is also sanctified by her sacrifice. She is hallowed through her suffering, placing her own needs and concerns to the periphery. Like Rachel who saw she bore Jacob no children, she exclaims, "Give me children, or else I die" (ibid., 30:1). And through her suffering, and her sacrifice, she is exalted, for the future of God's world, and the perpetuation of His words, lies in her hands. Thus, as the Sufi poet Jelaluddin Rumi says, "Pain bears its own cure, like that of a child."

And as her children grow, she loosens her ties to them. She nurtures and caresses, serves and teaches, and responds to the faint echoes from above that disturb their peace. She recognizes that many of the rules of her family will come into question, and she knows that some must even withstand flexibility. She helps her children to take personal responsibility for their thoughts and emotions (even the negative ones), and in times of crisis, she finds ways to make even the most difficult conflicts resolvable. And as her family grows in age, she shares her children with God, and with the world. Like Miriam who surrenders her baby to the great River Nile, the mother anoints her children with the possibility of attaining the greatness of Moses.

In sharing her children with the world then, a mother teaches her children the ways of society. She imbues them with social values and mores, and helps them to connect to others while still remaining independent. She rises heroically in times of crisis and need, even if those needs conflict with her own. For she knows in her heart that, as they begin to imbibe the lessons of life, and incorporate the skills of their youth, her children will one day move out and live on their own.

Thus, when we lose a mother, it is as if we are losing our whole world.

God and His imperfect cosmos come more clearly into question and we are unsure of His presence in our lives. The world He created is even more diminished now and, like a moonless sky, darkness is all we see when we look to the heavens. But just as man and God unite to create and repair the broken world, so too, are we summoned to repair ourselves in the midst of our sorrow and grief. Indeed, it is our very sorrow that forces the act of creation, for we must create a new "I," a new sense of self after our loss. This idea is illustrated through the words of a patient who survived a car accident that broke many of the bones in his face. After five reconstructive surgeries, he said:

> I feel like I am being reborn, like God is asking me to grow and to become someone new. But it's not just a new face that I have to get used to. Yes, when I look in the mirror I don't even recognize myself. But even on the inside I feel totally different. The doctors told me that I survived the crash for a reason, that I am still here because I was meant to do something great with my life. And now I know that God has great plans for me.

In our search for understanding, we thus discover our charge: to connect with God as we move through our pain. Like our mothers before us, we climb part of the way to heaven and look down upon the work that is still left to be done. Brokenhearted and bereft, we unite the past with the present, and we create a new way of being. In the words of the Rav, Jewish law teaches that man must create himself in the context of a living, enduring past, while facing a bright and welcoming future.

Thus, when we journey through the land of grief, we refuse to accept the permanence of all that is broken and lost. We honor the image of God in ourselves, and the mother within us as well. We refuse to believe that our mother's love is gone forever, irretrievable and unable to emanate from within. We learn that there is bravery in memory, and that there is bravery in partnership. With valor in our hearts, we take on the challenge to remember, to partner with God, and to create ourselves anew, and we carry our mother's lessons and love every step of the way. And if we listen closely, like Moses, we will hear God say, "Certainly I will be with thee" (Exodus 3:12).

# *Acceptance*

Dearest Mom,

Today marks the fifth day of your *shiva*. It is a short one, as tonight at sundown the Sabbath will begin, superseding the requirements of this ancient ritual. I realize that there will be no visitors tonight, just a short afternoon of comforters and reflection. I rise as I have done every other morning this week, unsure of what lessons you have for me to learn today. I quickly kiss Beth and the boys, who are all still asleep in their beds, grab my *tefillin* on the table by the front door, and make my way to your synagogue for morning prayers.

I notice that I am becoming more tired and weary as this long week of *shiva* draws on. Is this what is supposed to be happening? Are we, the mourners, expected to become so worn from the multitude of words and wishes of friends that we can't cry? Is this week more an exercise in distraction than it is in reflection? These are my questions on this early September morning. In my heart, I know there is much to be learned from this seven-day period of intense grief. And I realize that, as the shock and numbness of your sudden death begins to subside, I am beginning to accept the consoling overtures of more and more comforters. But with little sleep and two more days still to go, weariness and fatigue are also setting in.

I arrive to Morning Prayer services late, as usual. And instead of entering the chapel, I decide to sit here in my car. Prayer takes on many forms, I tell myself. So today I think I'll pray by sitting here and thinking about you. I am overcome with so many questions – and for some, I know there are no answers. Where did you go, Mom? How could you be here, so vibrant, beautiful and alive one day, and gone the next? And what about your things: the blazers you loved wearing so, your make-up, and hair spray, your crystal vases and miniature clocks? All of the materials of your daily life are useless now. Your beloved house, elegant and washed in sunlight, is also useless now. I sit here thinking about how many of us go about our lives naïve and unaware that, at any moment, all of it may be gone.

"I don't want to be buried in a plain pine box," I suddenly remember hearing you say to me.

"What, Mom?"

"You heard me," you repeat. "Your father was a religious man and that was the way he wanted to be buried. But when it is my time to go, I want a nice wooden box, maybe mahogany, with lining on the inside. And I want a pillow."

"That's not how we do it in our family, Mom," I plead.

"I'm putting it in my will. No pine box. You hear me?"

"Yes, Mom. No plain pine box."

I flash forward to the day before your funeral as we, your children, went shopping for your coffin. Shoulder to shoulder we walked through a large room filled with wooden boxes. Some were ornate and beautiful, hand crafted and gilded with brass detail. Others were muted and simpler, with square lines and wooden pegs instead of nails. And there lying all alone in the corner was that plain pine box you so feared.

"There it is. That's the one we want," Scott said.

"Mom made me swear I'd never put her in a pine box," I reminded him.

"Yes, I know," he told me. "But last month when Mom and I went to a funeral, she looked up close at the pine box and decided that it wouldn't be so bad," he answered.

"I don't know about that," I said apprehensively. "I wasn't there to hear her say that, Scott. And I remember what she said to me. No plain pine box."

"A pillow," Judi chimed in. "She'd be ok as long as we included a pillow."

An hour passed as we made our way through the maze of coffins, deciding upon the one that would be your new home. We finally agreed upon a compromise: a pine box with delicate, subtle curves at the edges and cloth lining on the inside. Not elegant, and not washed in sunlight, but it was ornate in its own way.

"She'd be satisfied," we all said.

*

I open my eyes to see that people are exiting the doors of your synagogue. I realize that I have been sitting here for half an hour, and morning services are now over. I start the engine of my car, pull away from the curb and make my way back to my house. And as I arrive, I see all three of my boys running on the front lawn, ready and eager to begin their second day of school. They are excited to show me their new book bags and binders. I sit with them on the porch steps and watch, as each one shares with me his pride in the new acquisitions of his daily life. I smile at the irony of it all, kiss each of them on the forehead, and walk them to their bus.

When I return from the bus stop, I enter the house to find that Beth has once again arranged the kitchen with coffee and bagels, anticipating visitors and friends. This is what is ahead of me, I tell myself, another day of honor and grace, laughter and tears. I marvel at how life continues to move forward, rapidly and with an eye always on the future. I climb the stairs, shower and dress, and get myself ready for whatever it is this day is about to bring.

Beth and I decide to drive to your house to greet the afternoon visitors that may arrive there. As she drives, I close my eyes and, once again, I am pulled into the past. I think back to the day of your burial. I know that grief comes and goes in waves and I forgive myself for indulging these involuntary and unwelcome flashbacks. Suddenly I am standing at the side of your grave, and I see thirty or more people gathering as we ready ourselves to perform one last act of kindness for you before you leave us.

I stand at attention as I watch your casket slowly enter the ground. Joshua, Jacob and Davey are curious. They place themselves directly in front of the open space that is taking you and, with sad eyes, blow kisses into the abyss.

The rabbi summons the four of your children near, hands us shovels and instructs us in our tradition to bury the beloved. Judi, your eldest, is first. Approaching the tall mound of uncovered dirt, she leans in and gathers the first spade full of soil to be placed over your casket. One by one, we each take hold of a shovel and toss the earth upon you. Shovel passes to hand, hand to shovel, as your delicate and smooth pine box leaves our view. Hearts pressed in silence, we bury you, leaving no corner uncovered.

The rabbi approaches and tells me to put the shovel down. He says that it is a hot day and we are not young anymore. We should "let the Union Workers finish the job." But Scott and I resist, holding tight to our shovels, for we are determined to cover the whole opening.

"We are not so old, Rabbi," Scott says. "We are here to finish the job that our mother started the day we were born. Stand back."

And at that moment, more and more men approach your grave, picking up shovels and tossing dirt into the hole. Your words echo in my ears and I know you are satisfied. Piles of soil rain down, trunkfuls actually, as, together, your family and friends honor you.

Stepping away from the heaving mound of earth we have sculpted, we stand together and recite the mourner's prayer, the *Kaddish*, exalting God in his merciful and infinite wisdom. We hold onto one another, moved by the solitude of your absence, and pray that heaven is a better place than the one you left.

"We're here," Beth says to me. "We're at your Mom's house."

I awaken to see that I have been deep in thought for the entire ride. Smiling at me, Beth stops the engine and together we enter your sunlit house. People are talking quietly in corners of the living room. It seems as if Scott has a few friends visiting him, and Judi and Robert each have comforters that came. Shoshanna and Henry, your devoted neighbors, are also here, sitting quietly in the middle of the room. They see us, quickly rise and run to the kitchen to bring us coffee and cookies, a sandwich. Their kindnesses never cease to move me, and I cry just thinking about the love they feel for us all.

"You look tired," Shoshanna says to me. "You've been gone for two days. You have not been taking care of yourself."

"I'm sad," I tell her. "I move from sadness to fear and back to sadness again. But I am getting through."

She looks at me with a slight smile in her eyes, and I know she understands. Witness to the changing climate of this intense and mournful week, Shoshanna sees that I am growing, that the light in my eyes comes from you. I tell her about the *shiva* at my house, about my late night baking adventure in your kitchen with your old recipes, and about how you visit me through the compassion of friends and the love of my wife. I tell her about the memories that keep flashing back through my mind, unexpected and assaulting. And she says in Hebrew,

"*Tochal, motek*. Eat sweetheart. You need strength."

I take the plate of food she offers me, walk over to the corner where Judi is sitting, and ask about yesterday and about the guests who came to pay their respects. I ask her if any friends came for me and Beth, if any interesting or different foods were delivered. I am curious about the evening prayer services and if the rabbi from your synagogue came to officiate. I ask about the dinner they all had and about how crowded the house was. And I smile as I recount my stories of *shiva* at my house and the endless stream of friends that came to pay their respects.

"We had close to two hundred people come through our doors in Roslyn yesterday," I tell her.

"Well, we had two hundred and one," she says. And we laugh at our competitiveness, and I realize I am happy to be back in your home.

Hours seem to pass and the sun begins to set through the skylights overhead. The overabundance of food seems strangely welcoming now, and the friends and colleagues who came to console my siblings earlier in the week now seem more familiar, kinder. Even *The Shiva Sisters* seem strangely comforting today.

Bewildered, I sit back and allow myself to ask questions for which I know there are no answers. I tell myself to accept the questions even if they make no sense, even when they sound like words in a foreign tongue. I soothe myself in the belief that, one day, some of my questions will meet their answers along a distant path. And I forgive myself for the many thoughts and feelings that keep repeating themselves inside of me. Like climbing a spiral staircase, I visit the same thoughts over and over again. And I pray that one day, I will be able to see them all from a loftier and clearer vantage point.

Soon it will be evening, I realize, and the Sabbath will begin. Tonight will be a quiet night in our house, I tell myself. There will be no visitors. This will be a welcome change for all of us after these last five days of *shiva*. Realizing that the boys' school bus will be arriving shortly, Beth and I say our goodbyes to everyone and make our way back to Roslyn. I am eager to spend a quiet evening with my family as the silence of Sabbath descends.

Five days have already passed without you. Yet in some ways it feels like it has been a month. I realize I am changing through this whole process. I see how my initial distrust of well-meaning friends is gradually transforming into gratitude and acceptance. I am grateful for the moments of peace I feel when I'm with friends who listen with an open heart. I recognize that we are all afraid, even those who come to comfort the mourners; I accept that some people will say the wrong things without meaning any harm. I am surprised by the sadness I feel when your house of *shiva* gradually empties, bringing the sound level to a murmur. I forgive myself for shutting down from those who try in vain to reach me in my sorrow, and I accept my need to indulge in memories of my childhood. I see myself moving from man to little boy and back again, and I thank you for the strength that your spirit and memory provide.

Platters of cold cuts, coleslaw and potato salad, left over from yesterday's *shiva* at my house, serve as our Sabbath dinner, and we eat by the light of candles. Joshua and Jacob are telling stories about their second day of school, and Davey is falling asleep in Beth's arms. The shadows cast by the din of the Sabbath light are dancing all around us, and we sit here, calling out the names of animals and star constellations that we think we see on the ceiling above. It is the end of another long day, and I feel you here with us, as we climb the stairs and tuck each boy in his bed.

★

Morning arrives quietly, and I awaken later than usual. Today marks the sixth day of your *shiva*, Mom, and I am fiendishly relieved that the end of this ancient ritual is near. I recognize and accept that I have learned much in this short, dark time, but I am growing ever more tired and weary. Sometimes, especially in the mornings, I ache for the sweet, mundane things that non-grievers get to experience. I miss the little details of ordinary life, like the sudden rush of panic I feel when the school bus shows up in front of the house and the boys' shoes are nowhere to be found, or the guilty pleasure I receive from sharing unimportant gossip about someone else's problems.

I am aware, too, that soon enough the world I am about to re-enter will expect much of me. My friends will soon tell me to "move on," to be "better." I've been through this before, when Dad died. And I know that people will long for me to be my once happier and lighter self. And my patients will need me to be strong and attentive to their own sorrows and to their own losses. Bills will have to be paid, traffic endured, and long lines at the bank and supermarket will once again have to be confronted. But as I sit here on this late Saturday morning in September, I still wish for a return to the mundane. I wait for a Saturday morning months from now, in June or July, when *shiva* and its attendant feelings of grief have gradually become a part of the past.

My thoughts are interrupted by a phone call from Judi. "Phyllis just called me," she says. "And she wants to take us all out to lunch today."

"I am not comfortable sitting in a restaurant on the Sabbath," I tell her.

"Well, she's coming out to Mom's house all the way from New Jersey to have lunch with us. We can eat whatever is left in Mom's kitchen if you want. But she's coming, so make sure you're here by two o'clock."

I am confronted by a host of competing questions. Why couldn't your friend come during one of the days we were actually sitting *shiva*? Why can't she come tonight after sundown with the rest of your friends and relatives? And why wasn't she at your funeral? But Phyllis was a close and cherished friend. She and her husband traveled throughout Europe and Israel with you and Dad, and I am reminded that you shared laughter together. I think about how she always made you smile, and how she brought out the crazy, silly side of you.

I remember one Saturday afternoon as a child in particular. You and Phyllis dressed up in old clothes you found in the back of the basement closet. Like Lucy and Ethel, the two of you danced around the living room, pillbox hats on your heads, lambswool shawls wrapped around your shoulders, and crescent-shaped eyeglasses resting on the bridges of your nose. I never saw you act as silly as you did when you two were together, and I reconcile that it is fitting for Phyllis to be alone with us today. I wake Beth and tell her that we have to be back at your house by noon. I tell her that your best friend is coming to have lunch with all of us, and that she has to make sure to get the boys to your house without me. She smiles understandingly, kisses me on the lips, and tells me not to be late for morning services.

I make my way to synagogue, and immediately see a friend who is saying prayers to honor the soul of his father. He motions for me to sit. Together we pray as members of the congregation hurry all around us. Hands turn pages as prayers are read, knees bend and lips motion words that some congregants don't even understand. Suddenly I realize that I have begun to split the world into two types of people: those who are mourning, and those who are not. I look around and wonder how many people here are mourners. I want to be surrounded by them. I long for one of them to look at me, to place a hand on my shoulder, and to say with sad eyes, "I know. I am going through this too."

After several prayers, the rabbi asks the mourners in the room to stand and recite the *Kaddish* – the prayer of benediction and honor that is said for the souls of those who have died. I rise timidly, and as I do, I look around to see who in the chapel is rising along with me. Slowly I see a group of twelve or fifteen people standing at attention. Some have prayer books in their hands, and others look straight ahead with no need for a book to guide them. I am drawn to these people, each and every one. I stare as one woman kneels, covering her prayer book in a loving and sad embrace. I watch as a bearded man gazes into the distance, and I wonder what it is he sees. I notice an elderly couple standing together, the wife wiping a tear from her eye. And I see my friend to my immediate left, three months ahead of me in his grief, as he recites the mourner's prayer quietly to himself. I join each of them and recite the prayer as well, and I am consoled in the knowledge that others are standing with me, where many have stood before, and all have survived.

At the end of morning services, I quickly make my way to your house.

The sun is high in the sky and I realize that Phyllis will be arriving shortly. I think about the morning that has passed and about the hours that lay ahead. I think about the mourners who stood together and around me, inviolate in body and yet broken in heart. I think of the friends who have tried to console me in these solemn days, some who knew how and others who tried in vain to reach me. And I think about your friends, those who came to pay their respects and those who, for whatever their reasons, could not.

As I pull my car into the driveway of your house, I can see that Phyllis has already arrived. Nervous yet eager, I enter and climb the center hall steps and see everyone milling about. Judi and Beth are setting the glass dining room table for lunch; Scott and the boys are in the living room playing with toys and laughing, and Robert is sitting in the corner of the den looking through boxes of pictures. And I see Phyllis in the kitchen, holding a container of chicken salad in her hands, and laughing as she places it somewhere on the table.

I am struck by how much she looks like you. I don't remember her hair as blonde, nor do I remember her wearing as much make-up in the past. I am at once frightened and comforted by the resemblance. Her presence here is strangely consoling, as I know she carries within her stories and secrets that keep your spirit near. I am drawn to her. I want to know what she knows, and I want to hear what she has to say about you and Dad and the days of long ago. As she reaches her arms out to me to give me a hug, I feel the ineffable weight of age and histories envelop me. Laughter, insight and reassurance roll into one, and I am comforted by the treasures that I believe can be found there.

"Tell me everything that has been happening in your life," she says to me. "How are the boys? They've gotten so big. And Beth . . . she's beautiful. I heard you are working hard. Your mother told me about the long hours and the great work you do. But I want to hear it all from you."

And that is how our afternoon passes, your children and your best friend all sitting together catching up on a lifetime of memories. We reminisce about the days we spent together in Florida as children. We cry as we remember the nights in Jerusalem dancing on the boardwalk in each other's embrace. We tell each other stories about the good years, and about the years that were not. She tells us about her daughter's recent divorce, about her grandson who has joined the Israeli Army, and about her life after Herb, her husband, died. And when we are through reminiscing, she stands up to clean the table, and accidentally breaks the bottom of one of your cherished kitchen chairs.

"Uh oh, there goes the rummage sale," she laughingly says. "Wait, I'll fix it."

And after several failed attempts at nailing the broken chair together, she screams, "Stick it at the back end of the table. No one will know it's broken."

Crying and laughing together, I realize how Phyllis must have helped you and Dad during your difficult years. I imagine her holding you as you cried about your daughter's divorce twelve years ago, and about Scott's HIV diagnosis twenty-three years ago. And I look at Phyllis as she stands here, today, laughing in your kitchen with a healthy Scott by her side, and I realize that her gift of laughter is part of what sustained you through all of the years we, your children, went on about our lives.

The hour is getting late and soon the sun will set. Tonight, and for the last time, your house will be filled with friends and relatives, the sixth night of *shiva*. Phyllis makes her way to leave, and we all exchange cell phone numbers and email addresses, promising to remain in close contact. I hug her one last time before she leaves, and I look into her eyes and thank her. I thank her for coming today, for reminding us to laugh whenever possible, and for loving you through the years. I wave goodbye, turn around, and climb the stairs to wrap myself in the fading light of the day.

One hour from now, your house will be filled with the love and attention of friends and relatives. One last night to stand together and pray in your living room, to sit together and reveal stories that are meant to heal and soothe both mourner and comforter. I close my eyes and think about all that I have learned from you this week. I think about how angry and unsure I was on the first day of *shiva*. Rising on those childhood steps, I looked around and questioned so much of what was going on in front of me. I was different then, for I accept much more now. I accept the different ways that people honor you in their sorrow. I recognize that some need to keep themselves busy, organizing food and feelings both at the same time, feeding their outside selves before they can touch the feelings that lie deeper within. I accept the friends who could not find their way to your *shiva*, and I allow myself to see that love prevails, even when distance and human frailty stand in the way. I even understand *The Shiva Sisters* better now, for they too are struggling to find a place for their grief.

I have learned that grief has no calendar. It starts when it starts and its end is undetermined. I see now that a successful *shiva* contains the eyes and ears of listeners who allow us to honor our pain without trying to "fix it," or make it better. I surrender to the knowledge that, without exploration, my grief would become toxic, eventually poisoning my mental well-being, and possibly my physical health, and my relationships with my family.

I search for moments of hope and understand that, while fleeting, these moments do return. I have learned that my ire and rage are only feelings – they too have a purpose. I have discovered that, once wrestled with, anger uncovers other, more acceptable and healing emotions. I see myself as a man climbing a circular staircase where feelings and fears are visited again and again. And with valor I continue to climb, knowing that, one day, I will see and feel all of these things from a more accepting point of view.

Reflecting on all of these things, I smile. I notice how close the word "*shiva*" is to the Hebrew word "*teshuva*," which translates into English as "repentance." I know now that the aching heart longs to atone for, as well as to accept, what it feels. I close my eyes and ask myself, what is it that I am repenting for? I recognize that all of us stray sometimes from the path we are meant to be on, and I think that each of us strays from the knowledge of what we have until we have lost it. I think about how fortunate I was to have had you as my mother all these years, and I ask you for forgiveness for the times I forgot to let you know it. I ask you to help me transform this pain into repentance and acceptance. And I return to you. Like a mourner exiled from a fallen Jerusalem, I know I will return.

The evening here at your house passes quickly and with loving conversation. Many friends have come to say their goodbyes one more time. I am comforted by your presence and I feel consoled, warmed by your memory and the lessons you have taught. I smile more tonight, hug your friends more intensely and respect the sadness of others more than I did before.

Tomorrow will be the final day of *shiva*. We will "sit" for one hour only. The rabbi will arrive and he will escort us as we walk around the block three times. He will say prayers over us, and one by one, he will take the rent ribbon, the symbol of our broken hearts, off of our left lapels. We will then begin our re-entry into the world from which we have withdrawn.

But tonight, as I sit here on this stool, I think of you and pray for your soul. You were my first love, my best friend, and my compass to a new love: my beautiful, brokenhearted wife. I know now that you have finished your work, and I see that you have done it well. We, your children, will be fine. You will inhabit our hearts, and you will shine within each of us, guiding our way through the dark nights still to come. Like flowers drunk from heavy rain, we have fallen. But we will rise again.

And now it is my turn to do what you have taught me so many years ago. With a heart full of gratitude, I stand. I see you in my mind's eye, lying weightless and timeless in your eternal slumber. And in my mind I lean forward and imagine kissing you on your cheek.

Feel my hands, Mom, as I brush away the hair from your lifeless eyes. And hear me, as I whisper softly in your ear:

"Sleep tight, *Mama shana*. I'll see you in the morning light."


## *Postscript*

Of all of the tasks that grief has set before us, reaching a place of acceptance is by far the hardest. For many, the word itself seems to carry within it the contents of an unfathomable goal. Indeed, thinking that we must "accept" the loss of a mother will undoubtedly leave us with feelings of anger, despair and hopelessness. As mourners, we never asked for this job, and we feel unprepared for the work and the struggle that lies ahead. How, then, do we "attain a heart of wisdom" and acquire an ability to accept our fate? And how do we face the inevitable when it happens to the mother we love?

Perhaps a more manageable approach to understanding the concept of "acceptance" is to break the word down into it smaller parts. Looking at the word acrostically, we can surmise that each of its letters carries with it a different charge. More specifically, when we "accept" the pain of losing a mother, we

> **A**cknowledge the existence of God
> **C**oncede to honor the task that God has given us (even though we may not like it)
> **C**onnect with others who understand our sorrow
> **E**mbrace our grief for as long as we need
> **P**lace our grief somewhere inside where it no longer defines and/or assaults us
> **T**each the world what we are learning.

The first phase of acceptance, *Acknowledgement,* may be the hardest, for in our darkest moments, we are being asked to affirm God's existence. According to Moses Maimonides, the great scholar and author of *Laws of the Foundations of the Torah,* man must know the basic principle that there is a First Existent who brought everything into being. For Maimonides, there is no existence without God, and there is no reality without reliance on Him. God pervades the world bountifully, even in our times of sorrow. There are indeed moments when we fear that God has abandoned us, concealed Himself behind a wall of obscurity, or denied our pleas for comfort and repair. But just like Nachshon ben Aminadav, who was the first among the entire Jewish slaves of Egypt to "plunge with his tribe after him into the waves of the Red Sea" (Talmud *Sotah* 37a), we too are being asked to hold strongly to a belief that God will stop us from drowning. Without a belief in the existence of a Creator, or a force that, in the words of the Rav, "fills everything and surrounds everything, causes everything and outlasts everything," we will not be able to plunge forward in our sorrow and our grief.

But to acknowledge God's existence introduces, for us, an essential psychological and spiritual challenge. For as fiercely as we run toward God, we equally retreat from Him. We ask ourselves, "How we can we live in a world without God?" and conversely ask, "How can we attach ourselves to God and maintain a sense of independence and self-power?" This dialectic, or pendulum-like movement of love and awe, is at the very heart of our development as human beings. More specifically, from the seminal writings of Sigmund Freud and Margaret Mahler, we learn that "growing *up*" entails a gradual "growing *away*" from the state of "oneness" with the mother (creator of life). But it also gives rise to a lifelong process of longing. This is because inherent in every new step of independence from our "creator" lies the threat of loss and a fear of annihilation. Just as the toddler runs away from its mother, but is always looking back to make sure she is right behind him, so too do we, in our grief, run from God with a silent wish to be re-united and consoled.

Thus when we acknowledge God's existence, and we reach out to Him in our grief, we find ourselves swinging back and forth between two opposite poles. We beseech God in His splendor (feelings of love) and we fear his magnanimous power (feelings of awe).

This dialectic is no better reflected than in the phrasing of Psalm 23, in which King David speaks about God in the third-person, changes his tense and speaks directly to God in the middle of the Psalm, and ends speaking about Him once again in the third-person. The beginning of the Psalm expresses the silent despair of David, who is searching for God in His concealment:

> The Lord is my shepherd; I shall not want.
> He maketh me to lie down in green pastures;
> He restoreth my soul;
> He guideth me in straight paths for His name's sake.

But in the midst of his mourning, David comes closer to God. He expresses an aspiration of the community of mourners who have come before him, and he reaches the point of an intimate conversation within an "I-Thou" relationship:

Yea, though I walk through the valley of the shadow of death,
I will fear no evil,
For Thou art with me;
Thy rod and thy staff, they comfort me.
Thou preparest a table before me in the presence of mine
    enemies;
Thou hast anointed my head with oil; my cup runneth over.

As soon as the sublime attachment has begun, however, the Psalm returns to the third-person, and God becomes the "Hidden One" once again. The intimate relationship is dissolved, and the distance between man and God grows. David, just like many of us in our grief, returns to speaking to the God who is concealed in the shadows of heaven, and he is blessed from God's distant place on high:

Surely goodness and mercy shall follow me all the days of my
    life;
And I shall dwell in the house of the Lord for ever.

In times of extreme sorrow and despair, love thus joins with awe, and our ability to affirm God's existence and to "cleave" to Him is met by fear and withdrawal. We who are mourning want to believe, but we may find ourselves caught in a grip of opposites. Our spirit yearns for the rapture of God's love, but the human instinct inside of us is thwarted by fear and uncertainty. The worship of our heart is connected with the pain in our heart, and the goal of acknowledging God's love and power for, and over us, becomes even more difficult.

But we must prevail. For in order to grow through the process of acceptance, we must wrestle with the ambivalence we feel about the existence of God. It is only once we struggle with our feelings and our beliefs that we can *concede* to honor the task that God has given us, difficult as it may be.

It is indeed a bold aspiration to rise from the depths of our despair only to concede to a God who asks us to carry such a heavy burden. For as mourners, we are forced to confront emptiness in our world every day. We question the choices we have made, and we live with feelings of longing, self-doubt and guilt all at the same time. In the words of one mourner:

> I keep thinking about my mother lying there in the hospice bed. She was saying something to me that I couldn't understand and I stayed awake for two days saying to myself, "What is it, Mom? What is it?" And then suddenly it hit me. She was mouthing the word "water." My mother was thirsty and she wanted water. But I wasn't allowed to give it to her. When I tried to reconnect her lines, the hospice workers got angry at me. And I knew they were right, because the water would only prolong her suffering. And now I have to live with that memory and that choice for the rest of my life. I wish she knew that I struggled with my choices, and that in saying "no" to her, I was acting out of love.

But our choices, and our ability to concede to God's plan, bring their own reward. Like Moses who asked God:

> Who am I, that I should ... bring forth the children of Israel out of Egypt? (Exodus 3:11),

so too do we ask:

> Who am I, God, that I should bear the burden of this sad and difficult journey?

And in our search for an answer, we discover that as mourners, we are not really that different from Moses, for we too are being asked to concede to a task filled with fear and turmoil. There is work to be done – God tells us – and with faith in our hearts, we commit to finish the job. And as we journey through the desert of our grief, we will feel God's presence within us. We will recognize that we are one of "the chosen ones," and that we must summon strength from within and from above.

The process of acceptance thus forces us to affirm our belief in the existence of God, and to concede to honor the job for which we were chosen. We are being asked to believe in a greater plan, and in a larger cosmos, and to have faith that God will be with us every step of the way. But in our sorrow and our struggle, we also require solace and compassion. We discover that we are in need of space and freedom from the statements and actions of well-intentioned, but naïve, friends and relatives. And we seek connection from others who truly understand us. In the words of one patient:

> Lately I find myself turning down offers from friends who want to meet me for lunch or dinner. They don't understand that I'm not the person I was before my mother died. They gossip and they complain about things that aren't really so bad. And they want to fix me and make me "better." So lately I find myself spending time with people who have also lost a mother. These people don't want to "fix" what is broken, and they don't judge me or the way that I feel.

Thus, we reach the third phase in the process of acceptance: *Connection* with people who understand sadness as we do. Connecting with fellow mourners or with a grief therapist, a psychologist or a rabbi skilled in the knowledge of pastoral care can help us to explore our feelings in a safe and controlled environment. Support groups have been established and designed for this very reason. Some are quite helpful because they give us a chance to speak a common language with others who are in a similar place. We can cry without being judged and laugh without being questioned. We can admit to being baffled at how the ordinary things in life – like the color of a new kitchen countertop or a dent in a new car – seem to matter so much to others but no longer to us. We can openly admit that we are hurt by friends who complain about their elderly parents; how they find it "difficult" to have to visit them, shop for them, and worry about them. Our friends don't realize that we would give anything to have one more day to shop, cook and care for the mother who left our midst.

Connection with a loving and patient listener serves another, more powerful, purpose. It helps us to tell our story with as much honesty and as much detail as we require. Every one of us who has suffered a loss has a story to tell. It may be a story of sudden loss, or a story of loss due to a prolonged disease. It may be a loss to a suicide, or a loss due to mental illness, neurological impairment, or dementia. Regardless of the theme, our story becomes our bounty to work with, to use toward growth, understanding, and soul-making. When we share our story with a compassionate listener, we gain mastery over the event. For most, pain leaves us feeling uncertain, and we are unable to act or proceed. Thus, the telling of our story, of what has been done *to* us, allows us to develop some control over the sad and unbidden event.

In addition, the telling of our story helps us to accept what happened without minimizing the loss. Those who have attended a house of mourning, or a wake, have heard well-meaning comforters offer words of consolation to the bereaved. "He is in a better place," they say. They smile and assert that "God gives us only as much as we can handle." But we know that these expressions of support are vain attempts to ease or minimize the pain. To the brokenhearted, they are empty words, and words rarely penetrate the souls of the broken and despairing. Thus, the telling of our story without the well-meaning, but ill-guided responses of friends who don't fully understand helps us to honor and embrace what truly happened.

Thus we reach the fourth phase in the process of acceptance: *Embracing* our grief for as long as we need. As it says in *Kohelet*; "There is a time to laugh and a time to cry," and a true listener understands that our time to cry has no prescribed endpoint or deadline. Some of us may feel ready to reconnect with the outside world shortly after a loss, while others feel that our grief is timeless and without end. In the words of one patient:

> People ask me if I'm "better." They think my grief is something that should be *over* by now. But my mother's death is not over for me. It didn't happen and then *just end*. Her absence is something that is happening to me every day. I am losing my mother a little more with each passing day, and this is a feeling that I will always have. My friends don't understand this. They think it's time for me to "move on."

In order to *embrace* our grief, and to give ourselves as much time as we need to heal, we must rethink the concept of "time." Spiritual man, according to the Rav, sees time as grounded in the realm of eternity. Thus, to a mourner who is searching for God's presence in the aftermath of a death, time is not one-dimensional, nor is it, to use the image of Kant, a straight line. Rather, "time" to a mourner is circular. There are days when we feel the weight of our sorrow drowning us. And there are times when we feel the strength and the vigor to rise. We find ourselves one day visiting with friends, attending a party or laughing heartily with others, only to wake the next day feeling lost and alone.

As Hope Edelman states in her book *Motherless Daughters: The Legacy of Loss,* mourning has no distinct beginning, middle and end. Grief, Edelman states, goes in cycles, like the seasons. Many of us start our grief work immediately after a death, but some tend to grieve in spurts. We start and stop depending upon the support we receive, experiences we may have had with a previous death, or the behavioral style with which we were born. For children, grief may not start for as long as six to nine months after an actual death. This is because children will feel safer grieving when the adults around them are beginning to show signs of improved coping. And as for gender, it is more common for the men among us to express our grief years after the woman in our life has expressed hers. Furthermore, those of us who have sought the help of a grief therapist, clergy, or a spiritual guide, may show signs of improved functioning well before those of us who have chosen to "go it alone."

While time may not be linear in a mourner's world, changes in grief do indeed occur. For most of us, the movement of grief is very deep, and it is expressed through our bodies as well as through our souls. Sometimes the shift from physical pain to psychic and emotional pain is insidious, and we are unaware of the changes that are occurring inside. This new and unwelcome burden has forced us to learn whole new ways of coping. We go from asking "Why did this happen?" to asking "How will I go on?" We move from disbelief and shock, to an unsettling recognition that "this is how it has to be."

One mourner has likened this shift to that of "trying on" a coat:

> In the beginning the coat was stiff, it didn't fit. It was scratchy and itchy and I noticed I was wearing it. I hated wearing the

coat. But as time wore on, the coat became more comfortable. It fits my body now almost perfectly, for it has become the ongoing vehicle of my relationship with my mother.

Other grievers claim that old grief, as opposed to new grief, is an "action-oriented" state of being. It is a way of being close to a loved one, a means of involving her in our lives. Some call it "mature grief," and they claim that it involves putting aside the physical, and moving deeply into the spiritual side of a loved one's essence:

> My grief is more than just a collection of memories. It helps me define who I am now; it gives shape and substance to the relationship I have with my mother. For without my grief, I could not have a connection to her.

Regardless of how we refer to it, the movement of time is entirely different for those of us who are mourning; and the shift from "new grief" to "mature grief" is an inevitable part of the process. Well-meaning friends and relatives who tell us to "move on," or to "get over it," do not fully understand this. They cannot appreciate that we will never completely "get over grief." But with the proper love and nurturance, we can, and do, learn to live *alongside* our grief, allowing it to be the unwelcome, but familiar, companion we carry through life.

Thus we reach the fifth phase in the process of acceptance: *Placing our grief somewhere inside where it no longer defines or assaults us.* Too many of us wake each morning and "trip over our grief" as we get out of bed. Our lives have become filled with sadness, and our sorrow has become the primary, if not sole, definition of who we are. We are no longer just a husband or a wife, a teacher or a doctor, a sibling or a friend. We are first and foremost "motherless." Some of us don't even want to be told that we "seem to be doing better." In the words of one patient:

> I got a tattoo on my right shoulder, and I wear it proudly. It has my mother's birth date and her name written inside of my family's crest. And I like when people ask me about it, and

what it means, because it becomes my way of saying "tread lightly, I am a mourner." It's like a badge, or a "Scarlet Letter" that is there to remind people that, even though I may seem better, I still have my pain to bear.

But in order for us to move successfully through our grief, and to learn the lessons that this life is trying to teach us, we must eventually find a place inside for our pain to rest. We know we will always miss our mother, and we recognize that her absence will leave a feeling of "heaviness" inside, possibly forever. But we also know that it is our job to keep living. "God has other plans for us," we say. "We have more tasks yet to accomplish." And one of those tasks is to attempt the process of "placing our grief."

Researchers and psychologists who study grief and bereavement suggest that the process of placing our grief is most successfully facilitated through the performance of an action or a "ritual event." Grieving children, for example, benefit from writing or drawing their feelings onto a helium balloon and then letting it go. The ritual of "sending the balloon to heaven" offers a grieving child a visual appreciation of the concept of death, and it also allows him a chance to express his feelings symbolically, and often without words. The planting of a tree or the naming of a garden, the creation of a memory box, scrapbook or photo album, are actions that we can perform at any age. They, too, will help us to facilitate the internal movement of new grief to mature grief.

Not all ritual events involve the creation of something tangible and precious. Some may actually entail the destruction of something that reminds us of the disease that "took" our mother. For example, one family burned all of the medical "roadmaps" their mother followed during the course of her treatment for cancer. Another mourner drove his car over the basket of unused medicine that his mother kept by her bedside.

Some rituals are guided by the way our mother lived when she was healthy and hale. In the words of one mourner:

> I stayed away from parties and celebrations for nearly a year, especially the ones that had loud music and dancing. So I

finally went to a *simcha* (celebration) last night and I decided
that it was time to dance. My mother loved dancing. And in
honor of her, I got out on the dance floor and allowed myself
to feel the joy that she used to feel.

The act of placing our grief may be symbolic, or it may be concrete
and literal. For some, it will generate a sense of relief when performed,
and for others, it may stimulate more feelings of sorrow. Regardless of
how it moves us, however, we know it is our duty to continue performing
the *mitzvot* (good deeds) that our loved ones can no longer perform. And
as we do, our actions and our deeds will become guideposts along our
path toward growth and recovery. More importantly, if we are successful,
we will learn that our efforts at moving through grief can be taught to
others who are grieving as well.

Thus we reach the sixth and final phase in the process of acceptance:
*Teaching* the world what we are learning. The transmission of lessons
learned through suffering is an essential part of our spiritual and emotional growth. It is different from the technical act of teaching where a
parent or mentor relays information, ideas and rules to a student or child.
Teaching these deeper and more spiritual lessons invokes the sharing of
our essence, our personal wishes, and the splendor of our relationship
with God. For the Rav, this transmission of wisdom is likened to a re-
enactment of the sublime revelation on Mount Sinai. In sharing what we
have learned, we become like Moses, who bestowed upon Joshua (Numbers 11:17) some of the original glory he received from his long journey
in the desert with God. And if we teach well, our lessons will embed
themselves into the depths of our listeners, and they will be revealed to
other students in generations yet to come.

Teaching the world what we have learned urges and impels us into
action. It forces us to reach out to others who may be hurting like we are.
Through our efforts, we may even gain wisdom from our students, for
spiritual and emotional knowledge does not flow in one direction only.
Thus, in teaching, we discover that we are not alone, that there are others
who walk a similar and parallel path, and they, too, are surviving. Teaching others will also help us to realize how much we have grown through

the course of our grief. Indeed, this type of "outreach" may re-stimulate moments of pain for us. This is because our exposure to the sad feelings of others often reminds us of our darker days. But it can also help us to rediscover ourselves, and to reflect on how far we have come.

Wisdom gained through suffering and sorrow is not ours to keep. It belongs to everyone. And as mourners on a path toward acceptance, we are merely guardians of the spiritual and emotional wealth that was given – painfully – to us in our time of loss. Thus, when we are asked by new mourners the age-old question:

> Why all of this suffering, what did I do that to deserve this pain?

we offer a different kind of answer. We share our wealth through benevolent moments of quiet compassion and timeless understanding. We sit in silence and we listen to their stories of sorrow, knowing all too well the journey that lies ahead of them. We tell them our story, and about the mother who is no longer with us. And as we teach, the "I and thou" blend into one. Teacher and student, master and disciple, we offer our light and emerge out of darkness, both at the same time.

Through it all we learn that the process of acceptance requires courage, for we must be brave enough to search for the wealth that exists inside of our pain. And in our search, we will discover that the reward is not in grief's "conclusion," but in the "process" itself. More specifically, when we acknowledge the existence of God, concede to honor the task that He gave us, connect with others in an embrace of timeless understanding, loving placement of our sorrow, and faithful teaching, we will see that our suffering is not a reflection of the absence of God's love in our lives. Rather, it is a confirmation of God's love in action.

# Conclusion

# *The End of Shiva*

Though the end of *shiva* marks the passing of one of the five graduated periods of mourning in the Jewish tradition, it does not mark the end of our grief. *Shiva* guides us and it allows us to express our sorrow in a time-honored, structured and loving fashion. But upon reaching its end, we discover that we are confronted with new tasks and new challenges. The world from which we had withdrawn now beckons our return, and the lessons we learned in the week of remembrance are only just a beginning. We have had an awakening of our senses, and a reminder of the fragility of life. We experienced the love of caring others, and the outreach of kind, and sometimes not so kind, visitors. Now begins the time to re-enter the world, and as we do, we must learn to re-craft our mother within us, and retain her meaning in our lives.

We have seen that, for many, this journey begins with the use of intellect. *Shiva* provokes many who are spiritually ambivalent to search for practical or logical answers to the question of suffering. This is because many among us are unwilling to take a "leap of faith" and trust in a universe that is filled with uncertainty. We tell ourselves that life is a stage upon which we act out our destiny; and we think our destiny is something we should be able to direct and control. But the process of *shiva* teaches us otherwise, for through mourning, we learn that life is full of mystery, and we are reminded that some questions remain unanswered.

*Shiva* also forces us to face the paradox of the human condition. More specifically, we know that every one of us is meant to achieve as much as we can, to grow, to move forward, and to improve our lives. But hardship and adversity inevitably appear, and we find ourselves retreating humbly. Defeat becomes our unbidden companion in times of crisis, and as we sit, low to the ground, we are filled with sorrow. But even in sorrow, we have a choice to make: We can choose to deny our fate (everything will be alright), or we can choose to surrender to defeat (we acknowledge the task for which we were chosen). *Shiva* teaches us that the second choice will bring us closer to our consolation, because it brings us closer to God. We are not "giving *up*," rather, we are "giving *over*." We are making a sacrificial decision to submit to a greater force and, in doing so, we recognize that our life, and the pain within it, is part of a greater cosmos, or a Divine plan.

Thus, through *shiva* we learn that suffering is impossible to escape. It cannot be suppressed, nor can it be rationalized or theologized away. Despair and confusion are normal and anticipated parts of the life cycle. But they are also the catalysts to one of life's greatest lessons, namely that sorrow is one of the channels through which God addresses us. In our times of darkness, we are being challenged to believe in a mystical force that will bring solace through personal growth, self-expansion and redemption.

Growing through our grief also involves a belief in the compassion of loving others who understand our sadness. We are being asked to open our doors and to receive the empathy of friends and relatives, a connection that links us to the wisdom of our forefathers. For just like in biblical times, when the sprinkling of ashes and water was required for someone to be cleansed from the impurity of death, so too do we require the showering of love from another to be freed from some of our suffering.

And in the process of connection, we find hope. We explore our needs and our wishes with comforters who care, and we begin to create goals for ourselves. We start to ask "how" questions, such as "How will I go on without my mother in my life?" And we realize that we even have some answers: "I will tell my mother's story to everyone I meet," we say. Or, "I will raise money to find a cure for the disease that took her." We see now that a plan is developing. This "plan" is our *hope* in action. Like in the first account of Adam in the Garden of Eden, we have been cast into a new world filled with challenges and fears, and we are determined to find dominion over them.

Some of us, conversely, refuse to ask "how." Instead we find ourselves lost inside the question of "why." We look inward and challenge our own identity. "Why am I being asked to carry this heavy burden?" we ask. Or, "Why did my loved one have to die the way she did?" In our struggle to find an answer, we await a catharsis, a moment of hallowed revelation filled with awe and wonder. We search the spirit within and look for meaning. This "meaning" is our *faith* in action. Like in the second account of Adam, some of us recoil and reflect. In our effort to understand the secrets of nature, we challenge ourselves to believe in and to turn to, something grander. We attempt to "know the Knower" and we begin to cleave to God.

And through all of our struggles we engage our emotions. We submit to feelings of fear, rivalry, jealousy and ire, and we search to find their spiritual antithesis – feelings of bravery, compassion, love and kindness. We learn that anger is one of the more prominent emotions during *shiva,* and we welcome it as one would welcome a teacher or guide. We learn that, when left unexamined, anger can damage a soul. It can confine us to our grief, causing us to withdraw and to remain isolated. But when we wrestle with our anger, we allow it to become a motivating force for noble and valuable action, as well as enlightened thought. Like Jacob in the Torah who wrestled with a mysterious angel, we confront our feelings and discover the truth behind them: That we are brave and afraid, strong and weak, all at the same time.

This dialectic, or pendulous swing of emotions and experiences, is one of the most healing parts of the *shiva* process. Through our long week of struggling, we have discovered that we are *in need* as much as we are *enraged.* We have looked inward at our anger and we have invoked its opposite, turning feelings of helplessness into actions that help the other, the "Thou," as Martin Buber asserts. And now, as we rise from our *shiva* stool and gradually rejoin the world of the living, we perform acts of *hesed,* or loving-kindness. We relate to our fellow man in pain and he relates to us likewise. And together, we pass through the multitude of life's hardships.

Our journey requires courage, determination and replenishment. Like a raging sea, grief comes and goes in waves. It challenges our sense of safety as it transgresses the borders we thought we had built around it. We now know that order and chaos subsist through time, for we have seen them dwell together within our world. Thus, we think of our mother, a woman of valor, who, in partnership with God, attempted to protect and shield us from the chaos and injustice that surrounded us. We remember how she lived only for us, her children, and how she tried to repair the world in which we would grow. We think of how she endowed our life with meaning; teaching us about *kibbud* (respect), Torah and God's many gifts. And we commit to continuing to perform the *mitzvot* that she can no longer perform, so that her lessons and her deeds can live on forever.

And with an undying spirit, we try to accept the path that we are on. Though we may never fully accept the death of a mother, we know that we must master the tasks of acknowledgment and concession; for in acknowledging the existence of God, and in conceding to honor the job for which we were unwittingly chosen, our consolation becomes closer than we think. God is with us through our dark nights of grieving. And with this awareness, we connect to others in an embrace of love and understanding. Our experience will forever change our perspective on life, for the death of our mother has intensified our appreciation for every life event yet to come. And with this appreciation, we will struggle to find a place inside where our grief can rest, where we can live *alongside* our sorrow without being defined or assaulted by it. And as we ready ourselves for the next phase of our journey, we will teach others what we have learned, for we have been gifted with the spiritual wealth that comes with pain and sorrow.

As a benefactor of some of this wealth, I have tried to share what I have learned. Through *shiva* I have experienced the power in surrender, the hope that consecrates faith, the *hesed* that comes from examined anger, and the valor that grows through the struggle to accept fate. Though I am still only at the beginning of the journey, I know I will prevail. And I pray the same is true for you.

Like Moses, who carried God's love within him on his travels through the desert, may you carry God's love within you, as you travel to find your own promised land. And may you be comforted among the mourners of Zion and Jerusalem. (*HaMakom y'nachem etchem b'tokh sh'ar avelei Tziyon v-Yerushalayim.*)

Epilogue

# How to Pay a Proper Shiva Call

O VER THE CENTURIES, several customs and observances have developed to provide the greatest amount of comfort to the mourner during the week of *shiva*. For readers who are unaware of these customs, I write them here:

Comforters who visit a house of *shiva* usually dress as if they are attending a synagogue. Some bring a gift of kosher food – cake, fruit or candy – that is taken directly to the kitchen (some send a basket of fruit or a platter of kosher food ahead of their visit), and some visitors participate in the prayer service that may be conducted during their short stay. The front door of most houses of *shiva* will be open or ajar, and the doorbell is never used. This eliminates the need for the mourner to get up and greet the visitor at the door; as he is forbidden to act as if he were a host at a social gathering.

Many comforters are worried about what to say to the mourner. Words of consolation often seem inadequate when visiting a friend in pain, and some comforters fear their words might make the mourner feel even worse. But when visiting a friend in need, all that is truly required is a warm embrace of love, or a gentle touch. Silence can be more healing than a room filled with well-meaning but misguided words. And since a mourner is not required to stand or greet the comforter who approaches, the moment of silence that is shared by the two will respectfully allow the bereaved to initiate a conversation about his loss. Some rabbis suggest that a comforter should not speak to a mourner until the mourner begins the conversation. As it is written in the Book of Job:

> . . . they sat down with him on the ground . . . and none spoke
> a word to him, for they saw that his grief was very great. (2:13)

There is an art to "not knowing." In particular, when a friend is in pain and he initiates a conversation about his feelings, it is wise to be dumb. Indeed, the more a comforter thinks he knows about how the mourner feels, the less the mourner will speak. And the healing power of *shiva* is that it allows a mourner to speak, and to be heard. Every mourner has a story to tell. It may be a story of sorrow, or a story of remembered joy. His story may involve memories of the loved one's recent death; or reminiscences of days passed when the deceased was healthy and hale. Thus, an appropriate and perhaps only topic of conversation when visiting a *shiva* house is the loved one who died.

A *shiva* visit does not need to last very long. The mourner will likely have other comforters waiting their turn to offer their love and support; and he may grow more tired as the visits wear on. The time for socializing and sharing news will return when *shiva* has ended. Thus, a simple but loving farewell, with the intention of checking in with him in the near future, is all that is needed. Upon leaving, religious Jews usually recite the following phrase as they stand over the mourner:

> May God comfort you among the other mourners of Zion and
> Jerusalem.
> *HaMakom y'nachem etchem b'tokh sh'ar avelei Tziyon
> v-Yerushalayim.*

Non-religious Jews, or visitors of other faiths, may wish to stand over the mourner and offer him a personal prayer before they leave, such as:

> I pray for your strength and your comfort in the days and
> months ahead.

No other words are necessary. In fact, the offering of words of "hope" may actually make the mourner feel worse at this time. Hopeful statements invariably include:

"He is in a better place."

"At least she's not in any more pain."

"It could have been worse."

"God gives and God takes."

"God only gives us as much as we can handle."

Words and comments such as these rarely help the broken at heart. Rather, they serve as a means of distancing the comforter from the bereaved. "Surely," we say as mourners, "there is no better place for my loved one than in my arms!" or, "This pain is much more than I could handle. God should know that." According to the Sages of the Torah, such comments may even border on sacrilege since no one knows God's ways or the true purpose of His decree. Moreover, many mourners may not want to hear about God at this time, for they may feel as if He has forsaken them and left their prayers unanswered.

Words of "promise" are also unhelpful; and they can be misleading as well. Such statements may include:

"If there is anything you need, please don't hesitate to call."

"I will be with you every step of the way."

"I know what you're going through. Believe me, it will get better."

While in the midst of intense grief, most mourners are unable to believe that *anything* will get better. In addition, their loss may have rendered them lonely and emotionally vulnerable to the well-meaning but sometimes naïve promises of others. Thus, they may take a comforter's offers very seriously, only to be disappointed if promises are unfulfilled in the future. Others may find the task of reaching out and asking for help to be overwhelming, and thus, they may never take a comforter up on his offer.

Hence, a "*shiva* call" filled with moments of silence and lasting compassion is perhaps the greatest gift a comforter can offer. Listening with a kind and interested ear, to the stories and feelings of the one who sits before him, is all that is required. And when the moment feels right, the comforter can stand and say a small prayer over the bereaved. Finally, with a loving embrace, a gentle touch, or a caring glance, the comforter can take his leave. In the words of one mourner:

> The healing power of *shiva* for me was in the listening. I remember that after my sisters arrived from various flights, we

all "sat *shiva*" together in my parents' living room. And everyone listened to us as we spoke about our mother. I trembled when speaking about her . . . I remember that I just spoke the truth to everyone who listened. No flowery words, just the truth. And those who listened . . . well, they helped me. As I write these words today, almost thirteen years later . . . I still feel my heart flutter.

Many who come to comfort the bereaved will be unaware that there are several prohibitions commanded to the mourner during the days of *shiva*. They are the same restrictions operable on the holy days of Yom Kippur (the Jewish Day of Atonement) and Tisha B'Av (the Day of Remembrance of the destruction of the First and Second Temple). It will be helpful for a comforter to know these proscriptions when visiting. For example, some comforters may wonder why the mourner is wearing the same clothes every day, or why he hasn't shaved his face. Asking these questions may be a source of discomfort for both visitor and mourner. Thus, the proscriptions are listed here:

A mourner may not work or do business during *shiva* (except in cases where it might incur extreme financial loss or public urgency).

He may not wear leather shoes.

He may not wash, bathe or shower for pleasure.

He may not anoint himself with oils (such as soaps, perfumes or cosmetics) for pleasure. He may not cut his hair, beard or nails.

He must refrain from having marital relations.

Additional restrictions include the hosting or greeting of people who come to visit; laundering, ironing or wearing new clothes, and the study of Torah.

In addition, visitors to a house of *shiva* will likely notice a special candle, or memorial flame, which has been placed in a prominent location in the home. This candle is lit immediately upon the mourner's return from the cemetery, and it burns continuously for seven days. The light of the flame is thought to symbolize the soul. For some, its presence is recognized as an antidote to the spiritual darkness that the mourner may feel at this time. Additionally, visitors may see that sheets or cloths have been hung over all of the mirrors in the house. While the custom of covering mirrors is of uncertain origin, for some it represents the diminished reflection of God's image, or the "disruption" of the relationship between living man and living God. For others, a covered mirror is a reminder that the mourner is less concerned with vanity, and more concerned with concentrating on his personal loss.

The process of *shiva* is a time of reflection. According to Maurice Lamm, in his book *The Jewish Way in Death and Mourning*, the spirit of Jewish mourning is the spirit of loneliness. It is a time for the mourner to dwell silently, and in solitude, on his personal loss. But it is also a time to rely on the wisdom of the ages and the lessons of the forefathers. "The golden chain of the family link is broken," says Lamm. And reflection through *shiva* can help connect the mourner to others who have suffered before him. It is a process that is designed to help restore the bereaved back to humanity, a time of great consolation.

The wisdom of Lamm's words is mirrored in the writings of many psychologists who study grief, for the journey of a mourner in the beginning stage of grief therapy is not unlike the first three days of *shiva*. Both are marked by hours of quiet reflection and loving understanding. The compassion of a wise and willing listener allows a mourner to express his feelings without censure or shame, and this is by far the most healing part of any therapeutic encounter. In addition, just as a patient needs to "review" in grief therapy, a mourner during *shiva* needs to review his story of sorrow, for this is his way of gaining control over the event. In the words of one mourner:

> When I think back on those days, I have unexpurgated thoughts. "Sitting *shiva*" for my mother was numbing, therapeutic, cathartic, exhausting, and repetitive. I felt like I was stuck in a "*shiva* loop" and I kept repeating the same stories over and over. In time I began mythologizing my mother. "Where was my real day-to-day mother?" I could only find the mother of the war stories, or the "injured" mother of the later dementia years.
>
> It was also an enlightening time as I learned more about my mother from her friends and people who remembered things

I couldn't know. I appreciated being cocooned in my parents' home, surrounded by those who honored her life. And, every night, as I shut off the light before going upstairs to sleep, I felt like I was Mary Tyler Moore flicking off the switch in the last episode of the Mary Tyler Moore show.

The process of *shiva* for some mourners, however, is very different than in Maurice Lamm's description. While meant to be a time of reflection, for some the process represents a time of distraction from the pain and loneliness that comes with loss:

> *Shiva* for me was part of the initial ritual that I had to experience in order to make the shift from "having an anchor" to "having *no* anchor" in my life. I was numb and in shock and incredibly anxious – my anxiety stemming from separation from my mother, my anchor. I was comforted by the *shiva* process, because it allowed me to focus on the people who were visiting me, and on the concrete things such as meals and services. I never had to think or feel. Going to bed at night, when everyone was finally gone, was the only time I thought about how my mother would never be here again, and that I was about to embark on a "cutting edge journey" I knew little about.

Unfortunately for many mourners, the *shiva* process can be so distracting that time for reflection and understanding becomes seemingly impossible. Some mourners will notice that their house is suddenly filled with the chatter and laughter of well-meaning, but misguided, friends and relatives. Noise can fill a space that often begs for silence, and friends may forget the solemnity of the process. Additionally, visiting a house of *shiva* can stimulate feelings or memories in a comforter of his losses. If such feelings are unresolved, a comforter will be less likely to listen to the bereaved with an open heart and a compassionate ear. This is known by psychologists as "compassion fatigue," and it is a process that occurs when helping others in pain causes a compromise in one's own ability to cope. The result will be a "silencing" of the mourner's pain through jokes, laughter, gossip or change of subject. Such occurrences become quite disturbing for the mourner to experience. In the words of one mourner:

> My mother's *shiva*: It was like I dropped a hit of acid. Kind of like floating in a Beatles video with "Yellow Submarine" wailing in the background . . . What struck me the most was that these people were at my mother's house eating bagels and lox and making small talk and plans for later that day. There were people laughing and joking, and truthfully, I was resentful. What was so funny? My Mom just died. And suddenly I realized that as much as they liked or loved my mother, their lives were going to be the same after they left my mother's *shiva*. My mother's death really only impacted my Dad, my sister, my brother and me. We were the ones who would, from that point onward, feel the terrible void.

Another mourner described her experience like this:

> When my mother passed away, I knew there would be a very large outpouring of support from my family, dear friends, and the community in which I lived for forty years. This was not my first experience "sitting" so I more or less knew what to expect. However, as in life, times do change, and technology gave me the opportunity to expand my circles. So the *shiva* became bigger than I imagined. My Rabbi, being a wonderful human being who was constantly in touch with my needs, advised me to find a "safe room" in the house. I questioned him and he replied that when the crowds become overbearing, it is advisable to take a break and regroup before coming back to the visitors. That was the best advice I could have received. You see, I was the mourner. Yes, many who visited were mourning too, but many who came to pay their respects did so out of the need to fulfill the *mitzvah* of comforting the bereaved.
>
> As a mourner, I found myself watching the parade of people who came to offer me their sympathy. Some understood my pain, others moved on to visit with neighbors or acquaintances

they hadn't seen since the last *shiva* call. It became a social setting, and I was left to grieve alone, and to realize that this was
*my* pain, and mine alone.

*Shiva* that follows a death due to prolonged illness creates a different set of experiences for the mourner. The bond between mother and
child is the longest in one's life, and throughout this connection, it is
our mother who is expected to care for *us*. But a critical or chronic illness changes the direction of this nurturance, propelling us into the role
of caretaker. Suddenly, we become witnesses to our mothers' weakening
physical and/or mental state. Feelings of hope and promise are replaced
by fears of powerlessness and moments of despair. Thus, when death
finally occurs, *shiva* may offer a respite from the difficult journey that just
transpired. In the words of one mourner:

> *Shiva* gave me a break from everything I had to do and sched-
> ule while my mother was critically ill. I was relieved the illness
> and the crises were over. This doesn't mean I was happy, not
> at all. But she had been chronically ill for a long time and there
> was relief that her suffering was over. In addition, when my
> mother was sick, I experienced anticipatory grief whenever
> the doctors came in and told me that "Today might be the day."
>
> Now, during *shiva*, I finally had a concrete space and time
> to focus on the reality of my mother's death. It was like enter-
> ing a "stop-time" zone where I was able to transition the loss. I
> felt the profoundness of her death in my life. I found that I was
> truly scared of the future: How was I going to move forward
> without my mother? What was I going to do without her?
> *Shiva* allowed me time to focus on these questions without the
> stress or fear of her dying.

Thus for the mourner, the process of *shiva* offers moments of solace
as well as moments of challenge. For some it generates a space and time
for us to think and to plan for the future without our mothers in it. For
others, it offers a time for reflection, honor and remembrance. For still
others, it is a time of distraction. Regardless of how we define it, however,

the week of *shiva* eventually comes to a close. Though the process of grief lives on in the heart of the mourner forever, Jewish custom dictates that *shiva* must terminate on the morning of the seventh day. It is usually not a morning of visits from friends or relatives, but rather a time for close family to stand together and reflect on the week that just passed. Many follow the custom of leaving the house and walking a short distance. This act is thought to symbolize our re-entry into the world from which we have withdrawn.

Whether we are mourning in the midst of *shiva*, or we are living through the months and years that follow, we know that our journey will be difficult, and that it will be filled with change. Some of us will experience moments of shock and disbelief, while others will feel the calm that comes from surrender. Some will suffer a loss of identity, while others will discover roles and responsibilities we thought we would never have. Some will turn inward and express feelings of anger, and some will reach out with loving-kindness toward others. Many will question their faith in God, and others will discover a renewed love for their Creator. And through it all, the love we feel and the lessons we learn from grief will be our consolation, our bounty to work with, until our fractured hearts begin to mend.

NORMAN J. FRIED, Ph.D., is past director of psycho-social services for the Cancer Center for Kids and the Division of Pediatric Hematology/Oncology at Winthrop University in Long Island, New York. A clinical psychologist with graduate degrees from Emory University, he has also taught in the medical schools of New York University and St. John's University, and has been a fellow in clinical and pediatric psychology at Harvard Medical School. Dr. Fried is a Disaster Mental Health Specialist for The American Red Cross of Greater New York, and he has a private practice in grief and bereavement counseling in Long Island. He is the author of the acclaimed *The Angel Letters: Lessons that Dying Can Teach Us About Living* (Ivan R. Dee Press, 2007). Dr. Fried is married with three sons and lives in Roslyn, New York.